First World War
and Army of Occupation
War Diary
France, Belgium and Germany

1 DIVISION
1 Infantry Brigade
Machine Gun Company
23 January 1916 - 28 February 1918

WO95/1266/4

The Naval & Military Press Ltd
www.nmarchive.com
Published in association with The National Archives

Published by

The Naval & Military Press Ltd

Unit 10 Ridgewood Industrial Park,

Uckfield, East Sussex,

TN22 5QE England

Tel: +44 (0) 1825 749494

www.naval-military-press.com

www.nmarchive.com

This diary has been reprinted in facsimile from the original. Any imperfections are inevitably reproduced and the quality may fall short of modern type and cartographic standards.

Contents

Document type	Place/Title	Date From	Date To
Heading	WO95/1266/4		
Heading	1st Division 1st Brigade 1st Machine Gun Company Jan 1916 To 1916 Dec		
Heading	1st Brigade 1st Division Formed in France 23.1.16 1st Machine Gun Company ::: January 1916		
Heading	War Diary of No.I Machine Gun Company For January 1916		
War Diary	Allouagne	23/01/1916	31/01/1916
Heading	1st Brigade 1st Division 1st Machine Gun Company-February 1916		
Heading	War Diary of No I Machine Gun Company For February 1916		
War Diary	Allouagne	01/02/1916	16/02/1916
War Diary	Les Brebis	17/02/1916	29/02/1916
Heading	1st Brigade 1st Division 1st Machine Gun Company-March 1916		
Heading	War Diary of No.I Machine Gun Company For March 1916		
War Diary	Les Brebis	01/03/1916	21/03/1916
War Diary	Grenay	22/03/1916	31/03/1916
War Diary	Maroc	31/03/1916	31/03/1916
Heading	1st Brigade 1st Division 1st Machine Gun Company-April 1916		
Heading	War Diary of No I Machine Gun Company For April 1916		
War Diary	Maroc	01/04/1916	12/04/1916
War Diary	Grenay	13/04/1916	22/04/1916
War Diary	Loos	23/04/1916	28/04/1916
War Diary	Grenay	29/04/1916	30/04/1916
Heading	1st Brigade 1st Division 1st Machine Gun Company-May 1916		
Heading	War Diary of No I Machine Gun Company For May 1916		
War Diary	Grenay	01/05/1916	10/05/1916
War Diary	Maroc	11/05/1916	20/05/1916
War Diary	Calonne	21/05/1916	31/05/1916
Heading	1st Brigade 1st Division 1st Machine Gun Company-June 1916		
Heading	War Diary of No I Machine Gun Company For June 1916		
War Diary	Calonne	01/06/1916	02/06/1916
War Diary	Grenay	03/06/1916	10/06/1916
War Diary	Maroc	11/06/1916	19/06/1916
War Diary	Grenay	20/06/1916	26/06/1916
War Diary	Calonne	27/06/1916	30/06/1916
Heading	1st Bde. 1st Div. War Diary 1st Machine Gun Company July 1916		
Heading	War Diary No I Coy Machine Gun Corps July 1st-July 31st 1916		
War Diary	Calonne Sector	01/07/1916	03/07/1916

War Diary	Calonne	04/07/1916	04/07/1916
War Diary	Barlin	05/07/1916	06/07/1916
War Diary	Wargnies	07/07/1916	07/07/1916
War Diary	Mollens-Au-Bois	08/07/1916	08/07/1916
War Diary	Baizieux	09/07/1916	09/07/1916
War Diary	Albert	10/07/1916	10/07/1916
War Diary	N.of Somme	11/07/1916	14/07/1916
War Diary	S. Of Somme	14/07/1916	17/07/1916
War Diary	Albert	18/07/1916	27/07/1916
War Diary	Baizieux	28/07/1916	31/07/1916
Heading	1st Brigade 1st Division 1st Brigade Machine Gun Company August 1916		
Heading	War Diary of No I Machine Gun Company For August 1916		
War Diary	Baizieux	01/08/1916	14/08/1916
War Diary	Becourt S.B. Bazintin-Le-Petit	15/08/1916	16/08/1916
War Diary	S Of Bazintin Le Petit	17/08/1916	25/08/1916
War Diary	Mametz Wood	26/08/1916	27/08/1916
War Diary	Bazintin-Le-Grand	27/08/1916	31/08/1916
War Diary	Mametz Wood	31/08/1916	31/08/1916
Heading	1st Brigade 1st Division 1st Machine Gun Company-September 1916		
Heading	War Diary of No 1 Machine Gun Company For September 1916		
War Diary		01/09/1916	30/09/1916
Heading	1st Brigade 1st Division 1st Machine Gun Company-October 1916		
War Diary	Brasle	01/10/1916	06/10/1916
War Diary	Frirevlles	07/10/1916	31/10/1916
Heading	1st Brigade 1st Division 1st Machine Gun Company-November 1916		
War Diary	Henencourt	01/11/1916	05/11/1916
War Diary	Becourt	06/11/1916	30/11/1916
Heading	1st Brigade 1st Division 1st Machine Gun Company-December 1916		
War Diary	In The Field	01/12/1916	31/12/1916
Heading	1st Division 1st Infy Bde No.1 Machine Gun Coy Jan-Dec 1917		
Heading	War Diary No.1 Machine Gun Coy 1st Infantry Brigade 1st Division January 1917		
War Diary	In The Field	01/01/1917	31/01/1917
Heading	War Diary No.1 Machine Gun Company 1st Infantry Brigade 1st Division February 1917		
War Diary	In The Field	01/02/1917	28/02/1917
Heading	War Diary No.1 Machine Gun Company 1st Infantry Brigade 1st Division March 1917		
War Diary	In The Field	01/03/1917	31/03/1917
Heading	War Diary No.1 Machine Gun Coy 1st Infantry Brigade 1st Division April 1917		
War Diary	In The Field	01/04/1917	30/04/1917
Heading	War Diary No.1 Machine Gun Company 1st Infantry Brigade 1st Division May 1917		
War Diary	In The Field	01/05/1917	31/05/1917
Heading	War Diary No.1 Machine Gun Company 1st Infantry Brigade 1st Division June 1917		
War Diary	In The Field	01/06/1917	30/06/1917

Heading	War Diary No.1 Machine Gun Company 1st Infantry Brigade 1st Division July 1917		
War Diary	In The Field	01/07/1917	31/07/1917
Heading	War Diary No.1 Machine Gun Company 1st Infantry Brigade 1st Division August 1917		
War Diary	In The Field	01/08/1917	31/08/1917
Heading	War Diary No.1 Machine Gun Company 1st Infantry Brigade 1st Division September 1917		
War Diary	In The Field	01/09/1917	30/09/1917
Heading	War Diary No.1 Machine Gun Company 1st Infantry Brigade 1st Division October 1917		
War Diary	In The Field	01/10/1917	31/10/1917
Heading	War Diary No.1 Machine Gun Company 1st Infantry Brigade 1st Division November 1917		
War Diary	In The Field	01/11/1917	30/11/1917
Heading	War Diary No.1 Machine Gun Company 1st Infantry Brigade 1st Division December 1917		
War Diary	In The Field	01/12/1917	31/12/1917
Heading	1st Division 1st Infy Bde No.1 Machine Gun Coy. Jan-Feb 1918		
War Diary	In The Field	01/01/1918	28/02/1918

1ST DIVISION
1ST BRIGADE

1ST MACHINE GUN COMPANY

~~JAN - DEC 1916~~

JAN 1916 to 1916 DEC

1st Brigade.

1st Division.

Formed in France 23.1.16.

1st MACHINE GUN COMPANY ::: JANUARY 1916.

Army Form C. 2118.

Instructions regarding War Diaries and Intelligence Summaries are contained in F. S. Regs., Part II. and the Staff Manual respectively. Title pages will be prepared in manuscript.

WAR DIARY
or
INTELLIGENCE SUMMARY.
(Erase heading not required.)

Vol I

Place	Date	Hour	Summary of Events and Information	Remarks and references to Appendices
			WAR DIARY of No I Machine Gun Company for JANUARY 1916.	

[illegible signature]

T2134. Wt. W708—776. 500000. 4/15. Sir J. C. & S.

Instructions regarding War Diaries and Intelligence Summaries are contained in F. S. Regs., Part II. and the Staff Manual respectively. Title pages will be prepared in manuscript.

WAR DIARY
or
INTELLIGENCE SUMMARY.
(Erase heading not required.)

Army Form C. 2118.

Place	Date	Hour	Summary of Events and Information	Remarks and references to Appendices
	1916 JAN			
ALLOUAGNE	23		No. I Machine Gun Company was ordered to be formed on 23/1/16. The strength of the Coy to be 9 Officers, 1 W.O. 140 Non-comm officers and men with 52 horses and to be armed with 16 Vickers Machine Guns organised into 4 Sections. The sections were formed from the Battalions in 1st Bge as follows:-	
			No. I Section — 1st Royal Highlanders (B.W.)	
			" II " — 1st Q.O. Cameron Highlanders	
			" III " — 14th Battn London Regt (London Scottish)	
			" IV " — { 8th Royal Berkshire Regt. { 10th Gloster Regt.	
			The Company to be under the Command of 2nd Lt. (temp Capt) J. ANGELL South Lancashire Regt, with 2nd Lieut J.C MURLEY London Scottish as second-in command	
	23		The Company is formed in ALLOUAGNE where the 1st Bge is resting.	
				Townley 4

T2134. Wt. W708—776. 500000. 4/15. Sir J. C. & S.

Instructions regarding War Diaries and Intelligence Summaries are contained in F. S. Regs., Part II. and the Staff Manual respectively. Title pages will be prepared in manuscript.

WAR DIARY
or
INTELLIGENCE SUMMARY.
(Erase heading not required.)

Army Form C. 2118.

Place	Date	Hour	Summary of Events and Information	Remarks and references to Appendices
	1916 Jan			
ALLOUAGNE	24		Devoted to organising and getting settled	
	25.		Commence training and parades as a Company.	
	26.		Company training	
	27		The Company strength is increased by 35 additional men who are to be attached to M.G. Corps from the Battns in this Bde thus bringing up gun teams to 6 men per gun.	
	28		Company training	
	29 30 31		Period of training – typical day's programme. 7-8 Physical training 9.30-12.30 Field Work + firing 2-3 I.D. Belt filling &c.	
			Weather period 23/31 Jan. Fine + warm	
			OFFICERS on formation. Capt. J. ANGELL. Lieuts. J.C. MURLEY J.A. ROYDS, F. LISMORE, G.B. COOTE, J.W. GARDEN, R. ALEXANDER I.R. BRUCE, D.N. WIMBERLEY.	
				[signature]

T2134. Wt. W708–776. 500000. 4/15. Sir J. C. & S.

1st Brigade.,

1st Division.

1st MACHINE GUN COMPANY :: FEBRUARY 1916.

Instructions regarding War Diaries and Intelligence Summaries are contained in F. S. Regs., Part II. and the Staff Manual respectively. Title pages will be prepared in manuscript.

WAR DIARY
or
INTELLIGENCE SUMMARY.
(Erase heading not required.)

Army Form C. 2118.

Vol II

Place	Date	Hour	Summary of Events and Information	Remarks and references to Appendices
			WAR DIARY of No I Machine Gun Company for FEBRUARY 1916	

T2134. Wt. W708—776. 500000. 4/15. Sir J. C. & S.

Instructions regarding War Diaries and Intelligence Summaries are contained in F. S. Regs., Part II. and the Staff Manual respectively. Title pages will be prepared in manuscript.

WAR DIARY
or
INTELLIGENCE SUMMARY.
(Erase heading not required.)

Army Form C. 2118.

Place	Date	Hour	Summary of Events and Information	Remarks and references to Appendices
	1916			
ALLOUAGNE	Feb. 1, 2, 3, 4, 5, 6, 7		Period of training – typical days programme. 7–8. Physical training 9.30–12.30 Field work Firing on Range 2–3 Judging distance, Visual training, Belt filling &c Occasional route marches & field days.	
	8		The London Scottish men (No. 3 Section) have been withdrawn from the Company today as their Regiment is leaving the Division. Our numbers have been made up by 16 new men from each of 8th ROYAL BERKS and 10th GLOSTERS. These men are however quite untrained and we shall have to commence an elementary class.	
	9		No. 3 Section is now composed of 10th GLOSTERS and No. 4 Section of 8th ROYAL BERKS. Company training & organising new sections.	[signature]

T2134. Wt. W708–776. 500000. 4/15. Sir J. C. & S.

Army Form C. 2118.

Instructions regarding War Diaries and Intelligence Summaries are contained in F. S. Regs., Part II. and the Staff Manual respectively. Title pages will be prepared in manuscript.

WAR DIARY
or
INTELLIGENCE SUMMARY.
(Erase heading not required.)

Place	Date	Hour	Summary of Events and Information	Remarks and references to Appendices
	1916 Feb			
ALLOUAGNE	10–13		Continued training	
	14		A Brigade field day in BOIS DES DAMES.	
	15		Prepared to move to firing line.	
	16		1st Division moved to the firing line. 2nd and 3rd Bdes in the line and the 1st Bde in reserve at LES BREBIS. Machine Gun Company moved by road, while the personnel entrained at LILLERS, detrained at NOEUX-LES-MINES, and marched thence to LES BREBIS to billets in the Specialists Area. Permanent H.Q. of the Company to be in LES BREBIS.	
LES BREBIS	17		Situation very quiet. A few shells fell in LES BREBIS in the afternoon.	
	18		Very quiet	
	19		do.	
	20		do.	Townley Lt
	21		Morning very quiet. About noon the enemy began to shell the gun positions outside LES BREBIS very heavily and used lachrymatory shells.	

T2134. Wt. W708—776. 500000. 4/15. Sir J. C. & S.

Instructions regarding War Diaries and Intelligence Summaries are contained in F. S. Regs., Part II. and the Staff Manual respectively. Title pages will be prepared in manuscript.

WAR DIARY
or
INTELLIGENCE SUMMARY.
(Erase heading not required.)

Army Form C. 2118.

Place	Date	Hour	Summary of Events and Information	Remarks and references to Appendices
	1916 Feb			
LES BREBIS	21.	(contd)	As the wind was E their effect was felt in LES BREBIS very heavily. During the afternoon the reserve Bde "Stood to". Shelling began very heavily at 5 pm. At 6 pm No I Coy was to relieve No 2 Coy in the MAROC SECTOR. Relief postponed to 8 pm because of shelling. Shelling slackened at 8 pm, and all guns reported relief complete by 11 pm. 7 guns in front line 5 in support & 4 in reserve. LIEUTS WIMBERLEY & ALEXANDER in charge	
	22		Aerial torpedoes were fired about 9 am about the left gun position. The M.G. dug out was destroyed, and Ptes SMART & MACDONALD were buried. It was impossible to recover their bodies. Remainder of day quiet. Snow fell all day.	
	23		Very quiet, practically no shell fire. Snow still falling. Difficulty was found in keeping the guns in action on this account.	
	24		Left sector shelled with H E at 9 a.m. Afterwards quiet. Inter Coy relief. Lt. GARDEN & COOTE took over. Still freezing.	Wimberley Lt.

T2134. Wt. W708–776. 500000. 4/15. Sir J. C. & S.

Instructions regarding War Diaries and Intelligence Summaries are contained in F. S. Regs., Part II. and the Staff Manual respectively. Title pages will be prepared in manuscript.

WAR DIARY
or
INTELLIGENCE SUMMARY.
(Erase heading not required.)

Army Form C. 2118

Place	Date	Hour	Summary of Events and Information	Remarks and references to Appendices
	1916 Feb.			
LES BREBIS	25.		Quiet day Occasional shelling. A mine was exploded by us at 7.pm. S.E of LOOS with the object of helping an attack on the CRATERS. The explosion was followed by a heavy bombardment by our artillery. Our M.Guns also fired. Little reply by enemy.	
	26		Quiet day – occasional shelling of MAROC or behind. Frost breaking.	
	27		Quiet day.	
		1pm	We bombarded the enemy front line for 5 minutes. They replied on our batteries. Inter Coy. relief.	
	28		Generally quiet – artillery slightly more active than usual	
		4pm	We exploded a small mine N of DOUBLE CRASSIER. Our ~~trenching~~ M.Guns opened rapid fire on surrounding trenches	
	29.		Artillery on both sides more active. Enemy obtained direct hit with 'pip squeak' on our right emplacement	
		11pm	Enemy working party heard near PUITS 16 – two of our M.G.s opened fire with effect	

T. [signature]

Instructions regarding War Diaries and Intelligence Summaries are contained in F. S. Regs., Part II. and the Staff Manual respectively. Title pages will be prepared in manuscript.

WAR DIARY
or
INTELLIGENCE SUMMARY.
(Erase heading not required.)

Army Form C. 2118.

Place	Date	Hour	Summary of Events and Information	Remarks and references to Appendices
	1916			
LES BREBIS	Feb.		Work done. A considerable amount of work on M. Gun emplacement has been done by the Company. Permanent sites have been selected by Bde. and strong emplacements are being built (heavy timber supports for steel rail roof + concrete surrounding)	
			Weather 1.2.16 – 4.2.16 Fine + warm	
			5.2.16 – 11.2.16 Fine, cold winds & showers	
			12.2.16 – 29.2.16 Cold, snow. Freezing	
			Leave about 9 O.R. per week	
			Lt. R. Alexander leave 4/2/16 12/2/16.	
			" J. Lismore " 11/2/16 19/2/16.	
			" J. A. Royds " 18/2/16 – 26/2/16	
			The spare men are billeted in LES BREBIS near permanent H.Q.	
			Transport lines in LES BREBIS.	
				[signature] Lt.

T2134. Wt. W708—776. 500000. 4/15. Sir J. C. & S.

1st Brigade.

1st Division.

1st MACHINE GUN COMPANY ::: MARCH 1916.

Instructions regarding War Diaries and Intelligence Summaries are contained in F. S. Regs., Part II. and the Staff Manual respectively. Title pages will be prepared in manuscript.

WAR DIARY
or
INTELLIGENCE SUMMARY.
(Erase heading not required.)

Army Form C. 2118.

Vol III

Place	Date	Hour	Summary of Events and Information	Remarks and references to Appendices
			WAR DIARY of No. I Machine Gun Company for MARCH . 1916	

T2134. Wt. W708—776. 500000. 4/15. Sir J. C. & S.

Instructions regarding War Diaries and Intelligence Summaries are contained in F. S. Regs., Part II. and the Staff Manual respectively. Title pages will be prepared in manuscript.

WAR DIARY
or
INTELLIGENCE SUMMARY.
(Erase heading not required.)

Army Form C. 2118.

Place	Date	Hour	Summary of Events and Information	Remarks and references to Appendices
	1916 March			
LES BREBIS	1.		Quiet - enemy working parties heard - M.Guns traversed their front line trenches.	
	2		LOOS CRASSIER shelled all day otherwise fairly quiet. G.O.C. 1st Divn inspected Machine Gun positions in MAROC SECTOR. Indirect fire on enemy's communications S of DOUBLE CRASSIER during night.	
	3		Very quiet - rain and snow.	
	4		Quiet day. No 1 Coy relieved by No 3 Coy in MAROC SECTOR	
	5		do. A little shelling in afternoon. Cleaning guns &c.	
	6		16 men per Battn attached to Coy for 3 weeks instruction.	
	6-8		Training as a Company	
	9		Preparing for trenches. Rain	
	10		Relieved No 2 Coy in LOOS SECTOR. Generally quiet. Some shelling near CORSE. Lieut I.R. BRUCE to Hospital (sick).	
	11		Normal. No 6 emplacement hit by pip-squeak - Tripod damaged ~~and sentry wounded.~~ 1. OR to Hospital wounded.	[signature]

T2134. Wt. W708–776. 500000. 4/15. Sir J. C. & S.

Instructions regarding War Diaries and Intelligence Summaries are contained in F. S. Regs., Part II. and the Staff Manual respectively. Title pages will be prepared in manuscript.

WAR DIARY
or
INTELLIGENCE SUMMARY.
(Erase heading not required.)

Army Form C. 2118.

Place	Date	Hour	Summary of Events and Information	Remarks and references to Appendices
	1916 March			
LES	12.		Normal. fine and sunny. Indirect M.G. fire on LENS RD at night	
BREBIS	13.	AM 12.30	Our Machine guns fired on enemy working parties at M5d 2 1 & M5c 9 2	
			Generally quiet.	
	14		Quiet - fine day	
		PM 11.50	Enemy working party dispersed by our M.Guns at M5d 5 3	
	15		Normal. German transport on LENS RD fired on about 7 p.m.	
	16		Inter-Coy relief. Generally quiet.	
			The work on the enemy's new advanced trenches about M5 c and d has been continued. Our M.Guns worried them all night.	
		PM 8.	Enemy transport plainly heard - M.G. fire ordered.	
		am 1. 5	German working parties at M5d 6.4 & M6 b 5.2 fired on and noise of work ceased.	
	17.	am 4.30	Enemy working party at M6c 2.6 dispersed with M.G. fire	
			Generally quiet - some shelling.	
	18.		Normal. Shelling on right of sector during night. Enemy working parties fired on.	[signature]

T2134. Wt. W708–776. 500000. 4/15. Sir J. C. & S.

Instructions regarding War Diaries and Intelligence Summaries are contained in F. S. Regs., Part II. and the Staff Manual respectively. Title pages will be prepared in manuscript.

WAR DIARY
or
INTELLIGENCE SUMMARY.
(Erase heading not required.)

Army Form C. 2118.

Place	Date	Hour	Summary of Events and Information	Remarks and references to Appendices
	1916 March			
LES GREBIS	19.		Generally quiet. Working party dispersed at M6c55 with Machine Gun fire. Indirect M.G. fire on area M11b & M11d.	
	20.		Normal. Short burst of artillery fire at 7 pm. in MAROC. M Guns fired all night on enemy's front line system. Lt. Murley to England on leave.	
	21.		Rain, Normal.	
GRENAY	22		Moved to GRENAY by Divn orders. Reserve M.Gun Company to be billeted in GRENAY in future instead of LES BREBIS	
	23		Reconnoitring reserve M.G. positions in VILLAGE – RESERVE LINES. Lt. Wimberley to England (leave)	
	24		Snow. Quiet day	
	25		Quiet day	
	26		Normal – some shelling in afternoon.	
	27		Rain all day. quiet.	
	28		Normal. Relieved No. 2 Coy in MAROC Sector. Lt. Murley returned from leave.	
	29		do. Indirect M.G. fire on enemy's billets during night.	
	30		Normal. T.Ms active on front line trenches	
	31		Normal. Indirect fire by night on enemy's tracks where movement had been observed. Lt. Wimberley returned from leave.	[signature]

T2134. Wt. W708–776. 500000. 4/15. Sir J. C. & S.

Instructions regarding War Diaries and Intelligence Summaries are contained in F. S. Regs., Part II. and the Staff Manual respectively. Title pages will be prepared in manuscript.

WAR DIARY
or
INTELLIGENCE SUMMARY.
(Erase heading not required.)

Army Form C. 2118.

Place	Date	Hour	Summary of Events and Information	Remarks and references to Appendices
	1916			
MAROC	March		<u>WORK DONE</u>. We have continued to improve the existing M.G. emplacements and sited new ones. The reserve line constructed by the division is very strong and a number of really strong M.G. emplacements are in course of construction.	
			<u>LEAVE</u>. About 5 or 6 O.R. per week.	
			<u>WEATHER</u> Cold & frosty chiefly.	
				[illegible signature]

T2134. Wt. W708—776. 500000. 4/15. Sir J. C. & S.

1st Brigade.

1st Division.

<u>1st MACHINE GUN COMPANY :: APRIL 1916.</u>

Instructions regarding War Diaries and Intelligence Summaries are contained in F. S. Regs., Part II. and the Staff Manual respectively. Title pages will be prepared in manuscript.

WAR DIARY
or
INTELLIGENCE SUMMARY.
(Erase heading not required.)

Army Form C. 2118.

Vol 4

Place	Date	Hour	Summary of Events and Information	Remarks and references to Appendices
			WAR DIARY of No. I Machine Gun Company for APRIL - 1916	

T2134. Wt. W708—776. 500000. 4/15. Sir J. C. & S.

Instructions regarding War Diaries and Intelligence Summaries are contained in F. S. Regs., Part II. and the Staff Manual respectively. Title pages will be prepared in manuscript.

WAR DIARY
or
INTELLIGENCE SUMMARY.
(Erase heading not required.)

Army Form C. 2118.

Place	Date	Hour	Summary of Events and Information	Remarks and references to Appendices
	APRIL			
MAROC	1.		SOUTH MAROC shelled during afternoon. Bursts of M.G. fire directed against PUITS 16 & surrounding houses during night. Lt. Coste on leave to England.	
	2.		Fine sunny. Quiet day. 4 M.G. emplacements for firing at enemy aeroplanes have now been completed.	
	3.		Normal. Front line M.Guns traversed enemy trenches during night.	
	4.	7.30 pm.	Heavy firing at 12 midnight from HULLUCH. M.G. fire on enemy front line & areas M10b M10c	
	5		Normal. Usual M.G. fire during night.	
	6		Normal. Slight shelling. M.G. fire on PUITS 16 – enemy have been observed at this spot.	
	7.		Normal. Our guns were active at night.	
	8.		NOEUX-LES-MINES heavily shelled. Capt Angell on leave to England.	
	9.		Relieved by No 3 M.G. Coy. Move to GRENAY in RESERVE. Lt Coste returned from leave.	
	10.		Quiet day.	
	11.		Rain	
	12		Normal. Heavy rain. Test occupation of all reserve gun positions carried out. The guns were all in position very quickly.	[signature]

T2134. Wt. W708—776. 500000. 4/15. Sir J. C. & S.

Army Form C. 2118.

Instructions regarding War Diaries and Intelligence Summaries are contained in F. S. Regs., Part II. and the Staff Manual respectively. Title pages will be prepared in manuscript.

WAR DIARY
or
INTELLIGENCE SUMMARY.
(Erase heading not required.)

Place	Date	Hour	Summary of Events and Information	Remarks and references to Appendices
	APRIL			
GRENAY	13		Quiet day.	
	14		All leave stopped. OC called back from leave. Heavy shelling.	
	15		Relieved ~~by~~ No 2 M.G. Company in LOOS SECTOR. Lively shelling.	
			1 man wounded on LOOS ROAD.	
	16.		Slight shelling. Enemy working parties fired on about N1 a 4.8 by M Guns. Heavy shelling of LOOS	
	17.		Intermittent shelling. Sgt. V. G. FARR appointed 2nd Lt in RE1.	
	18.		Capt. Angell returned from leave.	
		2.40 am	Enemy exploded mine between HARTS ~~HARRISONS~~ CRATER. M Guns 'stood to' till dawn.	
	19.	1 am	We exploded a small mine	
		4 am	Enemy's parapets traversed with rapid M.G. fire.	
			Normal. LOOS shelled. 2nd Lt. A. DUKES joined from Base with 2 O.R.	
	20		Normal. 1. O.R. rejoined from Hospital.	
	21.		Rain. Normal. More shelling than usual. Enemy M.G. observed firing. Two of our M Guns opened fire on it and silenced it. 1 O.R. to hospital.	[signature]

T2134. Wt. W708—776. 500000. 4/15. Sir J. C. & S.

Army Form C. 2118.

Instructions regarding War Diaries and Intelligence Summaries are contained in F. S. Regs., Part II. and the Staff Manual respectively. Title pages will be prepared in manuscript.

WAR DIARY
or
INTELLIGENCE SUMMARY.
(Erase heading not required.)

Place	Date	Hour	Summary of Events and Information	Remarks and references to Appendices
	April			
GRENAY LOOS	22		Normal. Rain. HAYMARKET TRENCH heavily shelled at intervals.	
	23		Fine. LES BREBIS heavily shelled. Unusual activity by enemy artillery. A lot of M.Gun fire by enemy.	
	24	2 am.	We exploded a small 'camouflet' off SEAFORTH ALLEY. More shelling than usual.	
	25		Enemy M.Guns very active – our M.Guns replied.	
	26		Fine & Sunny. Lively shelling in early morning. Normal later.	
	27	4.45 am	Enemy commenced intense bombardment N of LOOS CRASSIER with all size shells. Heavy bombardment until 7 am when it quietened down. Our Artillery replied heavily. The MUNSTERS (16th Div) reported enemy leaving their trenches at 5.50 am under cover of smoke. All guns 'stood to' and reserve positions were manned with M.Guns from GRENAY. The enemy raided 16th Div. trenches & remained in them for about 1 hour. Lt Alexander on leave to England. 2 OR to Hospital. 1 OR wounded. 2 O.R joined from base.	
	28		Lively shelling all day. We were relieved by No 3 M.G. Coy & went into reserve in GRENAY.	[signature]

T2134. Wt. W708–776. 500000. 4/15. Sir J. C. & S.

Army Form C. 2118.

Instructions regarding War Diaries and Intelligence Summaries are contained in F. S. Regs., Part II. and the Staff Manual respectively. Title pages will be prepared in manuscript.

WAR DIARY
or
INTELLIGENCE SUMMARY.
(Erase heading not required.)

Place	Date	Hour	Summary of Events and Information	Remarks and references to Appendices
	April			
GRENAY	29		Normal 1 O.R. wounded.	
	30		Normal.	
	APRIL		WORK DONE. Continued work on M.G. emplacements.	
			WEATHER. Fine.	
				[illegible]

T2134. Wt. W708—776. 500000. 4/15. Sir J. C. & S.

1st Brigade.

1st Division.

1st ?ACHINE GUN COMPANY ::: M A Y 1916.

Army Form C. 2118.

Instructions regarding War Diaries and Intelligence Summaries are contained in F. S. Regs., Part II. and the Staff Manual respectively. Title pages will be prepared in manuscript.

WAR DIARY
or
INTELLIGENCE SUMMARY.
(Erase heading not required.)

Vol V

Place	Date	Hour	Summary of Events and Information	Remarks and references to Appendices
			WAR DIARY of No. I Machine Gun Company for MAY – 1916.	

T2134. Wt. W708–776. 500000. 4/15. Sir J. C. & S.

Instructions regarding War Diaries and Intelligence Summaries are contained in F. S. Regs., Part II. and the Staff Manual respectively. Title pages will be prepared in manuscript.

WAR DIARY
or
INTELLIGENCE SUMMARY.
(Erase heading not required.)

Army Form C. 2118.

Place	Date	Hour	Summary of Events and Information	Remarks and references to Appendices
	May			
GRENAY	1		Our transport lines in LES BREBIS heavily shelled. Transport was moved to a more sheltered spot.	
	2		Heavy shelling at intervals.	
		8.30 pm.	We exploded a mine just S of DOUBLE CRASSIER after which 7 of our M. Guns opened a heavy fire on arranged targets. On return of raiding party 2 guns kept up M.G. fire on crater all night	
	3		No. I Coy relieved No. II Coy in MAROC SECTOR	
	4		Normal. Enemy working party heard near NEUF ALLEY & fired on – noise of work ceased.	
	5		Normal. M.Gun fired on arranged targets during day. Lt. Alexander returns from leave	
	6		Normal. Enemy blew a small mine N of DOUBLE CRASSIER at 2.30 pm. Followed by slight shelling. Enemy did not attempt to occupy CRATER	
	7		Quiet day	
	8		do.	
	9		Normal. Indirect M.G. fire on cross roads M17a 3.8 S. MAROC shelled in afternoon	
	10.	2 pm to 4 pm	LES BREBIS heavily shelled. Indirect fire on cross roads M11 b 1.8 by 4 M.Guns	
			Lt. Garden returns from leave. Lt. Lismore to England on leave.	[signature]

Instructions regarding War Diaries and Intelligence Summaries are contained in F. S. Regs., Part II. and the Staff Manual respectively. Title pages will be prepared in manuscript.

WAR DIARY
or
INTELLIGENCE SUMMARY.
(Erase heading not required.)

Army Form C. 2118.

Place	Date	Hour	Summary of Events and Information	Remarks and references to Appendices
	May			
MAROC	11		Normal MAROC shelled in afternoon.	
	12		Quiet day	
		11 pm	Enemy working party heard at M10c 9t. + We fired on them with 2 M.Guns all work ceased. Enemy T.M.s artillery very active at midnight	
	13		Rain. Normal. 1. O.R. joined from base	
	14		Dull rainy. Indirect M.G. fire on areas M11b + M17a between 11 am + 2 pm.	
		9.15 pm	S.O.S signal received. Company 'Stood to'	
			We were relieved by No. 3 Company	
	15		Normal	
	16		Quiet day.	
	17		Normal.	
	18		No. I Coy relieved No. 6 Coy in CALONNE SECTOR. Normal	
			2nd Lieut. G.W. Mackenzie joined from base Lt. Lismore returns from leave.	
	19.		Quiet day.	
	20.		Normal. Indirect fire at intervals on enemy's communications. Support + Village lines shelled in afternoon by enemy.	[signature]

T2134. Wt. W708—776. 500000. 4/15. Sir J. C. & S.

Instructions regarding War Diaries and Intelligence Summaries are contained in F. S. Regs., Part II. and the Staff Manual respectively. Title pages will be prepared in manuscript.

WAR DIARY
or
INTELLIGENCE SUMMARY.
(Erase heading not required.)

Army Form C. 2118.

Place	Date	Hour	Summary of Events and Information	Remarks and references to Appendices
	May			
CALONNE	21		Very heavy shelling all day. LES BREBIS also heavily shelled between the hours 4 & 9.30 pm Indirect fire on enemy's front line system during night Lt. Royds to England on leave.	
	22		Normal. Heavy shelling in some areas.	
	23		Normal. Heavy shelling from VIMY direction.	
	24		Normal & quiet	
	25		CALONNE heavily shelled. T.M's very active	
			1 O.R. joined from Hospital 12. O.R. returned to M.G. Base as they were quite useless as Machine gunners.	
	26.		Normal. Indirect M.Gun fire by 4 guns on enemy's billets between 1 pm & 3 pm.	
	27.		Normal during the day. At dusk the enemy commenced a heavy bombardment of our trenches	
		10.15 pm.	Increased to intense. Enemy attempted small raid, but were driven back by rifle & M.G. fire. A number of dead bodies could be seen in the morning. 1 prisoner surrendered to 8th Royal Berks.	
			No 3 Coy occupied the reserve M.G. positions in BAJOLLE LINE in view of an expected enemy attack.	[signature]

T2134. Wt. W708—776. 500000. 4/15. Sir J. C. & S.

Instructions regarding War Diaries and Intelligence Summaries are contained in F. S. Regs., Part II. and the Staff Manual respectively. Title pages will be prepared in manuscript.

WAR DIARY
or
INTELLIGENCE SUMMARY.
(Erase heading not required.)

Army Form C. 2118.

Place	Date	Hour	Summary of Events and Information	Remarks and references to Appendices
	May			
CALONNE	28		Normal. 1. O.R. to Hospital	
	29		Rain. Quiet day. Lt. Royds returns from leave. 3. O.R. wounded.	
	30		Rain. Normal 1. O.R. wounded.	
	31		Normal. Enemy working parties heard off BOYAU 10. M.Guns fired on them.	
	MAY		WORK DONE. The company worked very hard to perfect the M.Gun defences in view of an expected enemy offensive. All M.Guns had covered emplacements with 7.000 SAA on front & support guns & 10.000 SAA on reserve guns.	
			WEATHER Changeable	
			LEAVE 2 or 3 O.R. per week.	
				[signature]

T2134. Wt. W708-776. 500000. 4/15. Sir J. C. & S.

1st Brigade.

1stDivision.

<u>1st MACHINE GUN COMPANY::: JUNE 1916</u>.

Instructions regarding War Diaries and Intelligence Summaries are contained in F. S. Regs., Part II. and the Staff Manual respectively. Title pages will be prepared in manuscript.

Army Form C. 2118.

WAR DIARY
or
INTELLIGENCE SUMMARY.
(Erase heading not required.)

Vol 6

Place	Date	Hour	Summary of Events and Information	Remarks and references to Appendices
			WAR DIARY of No. I Machine Gun Company for JUNE – 1916	

T2134. Wt. W708—776. 500000. 4/15. Sir J. C. & S.

Rimmer [signature]

Instructions regarding War Diaries and Intelligence Summaries are contained in F. S. Regs., Part II. and the Staff Manual respectively. Title pages will be prepared in manuscript.

WAR DIARY
or
INTELLIGENCE SUMMARY.
(Erase heading not required.)

Army Form C. 2118.

Place	Date	Hour	Summary of Events and Information	Remarks and references to Appendices
	1916 JUNE			
CALONNE	1		Very warm & fine. Very heavy shelling by both sides	
	2		Normal.	
GRENAY	3		Normal. Relieved in CALONNE SECTOR by No 3 M.G. Coy. Guides were shelled at GRENAY BRIDGE. No 1 Coy to reserve in GRENAY.	
			2 O.R joined from base. 1 OR wounded.	
	4.		Normal. Lt Murley to England on leave. 1 OR to hospital.	
	5.		Normal	
	6.		Cold & stormy. Normal.	
	7.		Quiet day	
	8.		Rain. Normal. 2 OR joined from base. 1 OR to Hospital.	
	9.		Normal.	
	10		Heavy rain. Quiet day.	
MAROC.	11.		Relieved No 2 M.G. Coy in MAROC SECTOR. Normal & quiet.	
	12.		Normal. Indirect fire on enemy's billets & communications through night.	
			Lt. Murley returned from leave.	
				[signature]

T2134. Wt. W708—776. 500000. 4/15. Sir J. C. & S.

Army Form C. 2118.

Instructions regarding War Diaries and Intelligence Summaries are contained in F. S. Regs., Part II. and the Staff Manual respectively. Title pages will be prepared in manuscript.

WAR DIARY
or
INTELLIGENCE SUMMARY.
(Erase heading not required.)

Place	Date	Hour	Summary of Events and Information	Remarks and references to Appendices
	1916 JUNE			
MAROC	13		Rain. Normal.	
		5.30 pm	We blew a mine in TRIANGLE. Heavy M.G. fire in vicinity from all Machine Guns.	
			Bursts of M.G. fire on this area all night. 1 OR to Hospital.	
		8.47 pm	concentrated M.G. fire on M 4 d 2.0	
	14.		Rain. Our Machine Guns fired a considerable number of rounds in reply to enemy M.Guns which were very active.	
	15.		Very quiet. M.Gun fire on enemy parapets during night.	
			2 O.R joined from base.	
	16.		Lively shelling. 8 pm to 11 pm front line trench near NEUF ALLEY.	
		9.25 pm	An enemy Machine Gun was seen firing from trench in front of PUITS 16. We opened fire on it with 2 of our M.Guns and silenced it.	
			1 OR joined from Hospital.	
	17		Heavy shelling of trenches. M.Gun fire against enemy trenches S. of LENS Rd where enemy are working on their wire	
		6 pm.	Shell dropped in horse lines LES BREBIS killing 2 men. 2 OR killed 3 OR wounded	
	18		Fair amount of shelling. M.Guns fired all night.	
	19		Normal – relieved by No 2 Coy in MAROC SECTOR. 3 OR wounded.	[signature]

T2134. Wt. W708—776. 500000. 4/15. Sir J. C. & S.

Instructions regarding War Diaries and Intelligence Summaries are contained in F. S. Regs., Part II. and the Staff Manual respectively. Title pages will be prepared in manuscript.

WAR DIARY
or
INTELLIGENCE SUMMARY.
(Erase heading not required.)

Army Form C. 2118

Place	Date	Hour	Summary of Events and Information	Remarks and references to Appendices
	JUNE			
GRENAY	20		Normal.	
	21.		Normal. 1 OR joined from base.	
	22		Normal	
	23		Quiet day. Relieved No 3 M.G. Coy in CALONNE SECTOR.	
	24		Normal. 4 Officers from 121st Bge. M.G. Coy attached for instruction.	
	25		Stormy. Normal. Our Machine Guns were very active during the night. Enemy's front line trenches traversed, and indirect fire on roads behind his lines. 1 OR wounded. 1 OR to Hospital (sick)	
	26		1. OR to Hospital	
			Commencement of 1st Division activities.	
		9-12 am 12 noon 1 to 6 pm	Machine gun activity directed towards concentrated fire in conjunction with artillery on enemy's billets + communications with long range indirect fire.	See APPENDIX JUNE I.
			Our M.Guns co-operated with MUNSTERS in raid on German trenches. British shelling of front line from M15c 2.2. to M15c 8.4 between 4.30 pm and 8.30 pm.	

[signature]

T2134. Wt. W708—776. 500000. 4/15. Sir J. C. & S.

Instructions regarding War Diaries and Intelligence Summaries are contained in F. S. Regs., Part II. and the Staff Manual respectively. Title pages will be prepared in manuscript.

WAR DIARY
or
INTELLIGENCE SUMMARY.
(Erase heading not required.)

Army Form C. 2118.

Place	Date	Hour	Summary of Events and Information	Remarks and references to Appendices
	1916 JUNE			
CALONNE	27	am 1.14	In conjunction with infantry & artillery 10 of our M.Guns opened rapid fire on enemy's front line system, and houses and roads behind their lines and continued firing in bursts until 1.30 am. This fire seemed to worry the enemy, as he replied vigorously with M.Guns and rifle fire.	
			Generally lively during day	
		9 pm to 9.10 pm, 9.15 to 9.16 pm	Intense Machine Gun fire directed during these periods on enemy's support & reserve lines in neighbourhood of M 20 d ½ 5 and on their front line to N & S of this point.	
		11 pm to 2 am	All Machine Guns in the line fired 100 rounds every 20 minutes between these hours on enemy's front line system & points behind their lines.	
		3 am to 3.10 am	Heavy Machine Gun fire was directed against enemy's trenches at M 21 a 4.5 and surrounding trenches.	
			During day & night the enemy shelled our trenches heavily – two direct hits were obtained on 2 M.G. emplacements by 4.2 shells – emplacements wrecked, but guns untouched.	

[signature illegible]

T2134. Wt. W708—776. 500000. 4/15. Sir J. C. & S.

Army Form C. 2118.

Instructions regarding War Diaries and Intelligence Summaries are contained in F. S. Regs., Part II. and the Staff Manual respectively. Title pages will be prepared in manuscript.

WAR DIARY
or
INTELLIGENCE SUMMARY.
(Erase heading not required.)

Place	Date	Hour	Summary of Events and Information	Remarks and references to Appendices
	1916 June			
CALONNE	28		Generally lively. During the day our Machine Guns directed fire on enemy's billets & communications. All night certain guns fired on gaps in enemy's wire which he has been unable to repair where destroyed by our artillery fire & T.Ms	
		8.30 pm.	Heavy M.Gun fire by 6 guns on selected points.	
		11.15 pm.	Co-operation by heavy M.Gun fire with enterprise on our ~~left~~ right	
	29	1.14 - 1.17 1.20 - 1.23 1.27 - 1.30	All guns fired on M10b M16b M16c M16d. during these periods	
			Indirect M.Gun fire on enemy billets during the day.	
		8.30 pm.	In conjunction with T.Ms our Machine Guns opened rapid fire for 10 minutes on the following points:- German front line between RAILWAY M15b 6½.2 and PUITS 16 bis. Reserve trenches in rear and on either side of sap M15b 6.1, CITE DES CHAMPS GRENELLES.	
			No Machine Gun fire after 9 pm.	

T2134. Wt. W708—776. 500000. 4/15. Sir J. C. & S.

Army Form C. 2118.

Instructions regarding War Diaries and Intelligence Summaries are contained in F. S. Regs., Part II. and the Staff Manual respectively. Title pages will be prepared in manuscript.

WAR DIARY
or
INTELLIGENCE SUMMARY.
(Erase heading not required.)

Place	Date	Hour	Summary of Events and Information	Remarks and references to Appendices
	1916 June			
CALONNE	30.		Indirect fire by Machine Guns on enemy's billets during the day. The gaps in the enemy's wire were fired on continually during the night, except when our patrols were out between 10.30 pm & midnight.	
	~~11pm~~		Very little retaliation by enemy.	
	JUNE		Generally = During later part of the month the enemy were continually worried, and must have been expecting big attacks by us	

[signature]

T2134. Wt. W708—776. 500000. 4/15. Sir J. C. & S.

Instructions regarding War Diaries and Intelligence Summaries are contained in F. S. Regs., Part II. and the Staff Manual respectively. Title pages will be prepared in manuscript.

WAR DIARY
or
INTELLIGENCE SUMMARY.
(Erase heading not required.)

Army Form C. 2118.

Place	Date	Hour	Summary of Events and Information	Remarks and references to Appendices
			APPENDIX JUNE 1916 I	
	JUNE			
CALONNE	26.		Report on Machine Gun Co. operation in MUNSTER raid.	
			12 Machine Guns were moved to specially prepared positions, and fired at ranges varying from 900 to 2400 yards (also 2 guns firing from our front line) and traversing the enemys parapets on each side of the piece of trench to be raided – fire was continuous during the raid & these 2 guns fired 7000 rounds between them). The long range guns fired at enemy's support line, and 3 guns were clamped on the communicating trenches leading to the part of trench to be raided.	
			All guns fired excellently and about 20.000 round SAA were fired while the raid lasted. The enemy's retaliation was heavy. Three enemy M.Guns were observed firing and one of our guns especially detailed for this purpose engaged them.	
			The attacking force spoke very highly of the M.Gun fire and said it gave them a feeling of confidence to hear the bullets going over their heads towards the enemy.	[signature]

T2134. Wt. W708–776. 500000. 4/15. Sir J. C. & S.

1st Bde.
1st Div.

WAR
DIARY

1st MACHINE GUN COMPANY.

JULY 1916.

Instructions regarding War Diaries and Intelligence Summaries are contained in F. S. Regs., Part II. and the Staff Manual respectively. Title pages will be prepared in manuscript.

WAR DIARY
or
INTELLIGENCE SUMMARY.
(Erase heading not required.)

Army Form C. 2118.

Vol 7

Place	Date	Hour	Summary of Events and Information	Remarks and references to Appendices
			WAR DIARY No I COY MACHINE GUN CORPS JULY 1st - JULY 31st 1916	

T2134. Wt. W708—776. 500000. 4/15. Sir J. C. & S.

Army Form C. 2118.

Instructions regarding War Diaries and Intelligence Summaries are contained in F. S. Regs., Part II. and the Staff Manual respectively. Title pages will be prepared in manuscript.

WAR DIARY
or
INTELLIGENCE SUMMARY.
(Erase heading not required.)

Place	Date	Hour	Summary of Events and Information	Remarks and references to Appendices
	July			
CALONNE SECTOR	1		General activity. Indirect M.G. fire on enemy's billets during day. Lively retaliation by enemy. A good deal of work was done on M.G. emplacements	
		10 pm to 12 mid.	Heavy M.G. fire directed towards PUITS 16 bis and surrounding trenches	
		9.53 pm	Enemy blew a mine opposite centre Company.	
			Lieut D.N. WIMBERLEY left No I Coy and joined No 2 Coy as Second-in-Command.	
"	2		A quieter day than yesterday	
		1 am to 3 am	Short bursts of M.G. fire during this period on enemy's front line system. Enemy retaliated with 'pip-squeaks' and occasional bursts of M.G. fire. DOWTY'S POST received a lot of attention. The two M.G.s here were continually shifted.	
		8.30 pm	Intense M.G. fire on different points in conjunction with artillery & Infantry strafe.	
"	3		Normal.	
		1 am to 3 am	Enemy shelled VILLAGE LINE and roads to CALONNE with 4.2's & shrapnel	
			New M.G. emplacements in Support line completed	[signature]

T2134. Wt. W708—776. 500000. 4/15. Sir J. C. & S.

Army Form C. 2118.

Instructions regarding War Diaries and Intelligence Summaries are contained in F. S. Regs., Part II. and the Staff Manual respectively. Title pages will be prepared in manuscript.

WAR DIARY
or
INTELLIGENCE SUMMARY.
(Erase heading not required.)

Place	Date	Hour	Summary of Events and Information	Remarks and references to Appendices
	July			
CALONNE	4		Relieved in CALONNE SECTOR by 119th Bge. M.G. Coy. Company left LES BREBIS 1 pm and moved to BOIS D'OHLAIN, BARLIN arrived 4 pm - bivouac in Wood	
BARLIN	5		General cleaning of Camp & equipment.	
			Lieut H. RIDLER joined from Base 3. O.R. to Hospital	
	6	2.30 am	Company moved to FOUQUEREIL STN. arrived 6 am, entrained by 7.15 am. Engine of train left rails so did not start until 1 pm. Detrained at DOULLENS STN. 6 pm marched to WARGNIES - arrived 11.30 pm. 3. OR joined from Base.	
WARGNIES	7		Very heavy rain all day - men inspected and guns cleaned. Company moved at 7 pm for MOLLENS-AU-BOIS arrived 11 pm billeted in village	
MOLLENS-AU-BOIS	8		Company less transport moved to BAIZIEUX at 8 pm arrived 11.30 pm. Transport moved 9 pm arrived 1 am 9/7/16.	
BAIZIEUX	9		Left BAIZIEUX for ALBERT at 9.36 pm arrived 11.50 pm. Billeted near ALBERT STN.	[signature]

T2134. Wt. W708—776. 500000. 4/15. Sir J. C. & S.

Instructions regarding War Diaries and Intelligence Summaries are contained in F. S. Regs., Part II. and the Staff Manual respectively. Title pages will be prepared in manuscript.

WAR DIARY
or
INTELLIGENCE SUMMARY.
(Erase heading not required.)

Army Form C. 2118.

Place	Date	Hour	Summary of Events and Information	Remarks and references to Appendices
	JULY		Reference Map - French Map. Sheet 57D S.E.	
ALBERT	10		Company moved from ALBERT 6 pm. arrived BECOURT WOOD 7.30 pm.	
do.			Coy. H.Q. BECOURT WOOD O.C. at advanced H.Q. SUNKEN RD X 27 b	
			12 M. Guns moved up to relieve 68th Bde. M.G. Coy under	
			Lts GARDEN, LISMORE & DUKES and occupied positions behind & to	
			S. of CONTALMAISON — 4 guns in reserve on limbers in BECOURT WOOD	
			Road to CONTALMAISON very heavily shelled and relief delayed.	
N. of SOMME	11	1.15 am	4 guns moved into CONTALMAISON and relieved 69th Bde. M.G. Coy	
		4 pm.	Parties of enemy observed about X 10 b, X 11 a — our M. Guns	
			fired on them with effect.	
			Very heavy shelling on both sides today.	
			1 O.R. rejoined from Hospital 2 O.R. wounded.	
			Our guns are occupying the following positions — X 22 b 8.8. X 23 a 1.9	
			X 22 b 8.4, X 22 b 5.5, X 16 d 6.0, X 22 b 7.1, X 16 d 9.8, X 17 c 3.5,	
			X 17 c 1.4, X 16 d 8½.2. 6 guns in reserve under C.O.	
"	12		Lieut. COOTE, MACKENZIE & RIDLER relieved before mentioned Officers.	
			Situation not quite so lively	[signature]

T2134. Wt. W708—776. 500000. 4/15. Sir J. C. & S.

Army Form C. 2118.

WAR DIARY
or
INTELLIGENCE SUMMARY.
(Erase heading not required.)

Instructions regarding War Diaries and Intelligence Summaries are contained in F. S. Regs., Part II. and the Staff Manual respectively. Title pages will be prepared in manuscript.

Place	Date	Hour	Summary of Events and Information	Remarks and references to Appendices
	JULY		Map reference - Trench Map 57D SE	
N. of SOMME	12	8 am.	Party of 50 to 100 of enemy observed about X 11 d — M.Guns opened fire and killed a lot of them. Present positions of guns:- as before, except X 16 b 4 4, X 16 b 8 4, (2nd) X 21 d 7.6, X 16 a 5.4, X 16 a 1.3 — two of these guns were moved up from reserve the remainder from X 22 b	
			Lts GARDEN & LISMORE moved up line to take charge of guns to be pushed forward.	
"	13		Very lively shelling — one M.G. knocked out by shell fire in CONTALMAISON	
			2 O.R. to wounded.	
"	14	2.30 am.	Our M.Guns have occupied positions in CONTALMAISON VILLA and LOWER WOOD in conjunction with patrols sent out by Brigade	
		4 am	Our M.G.s fired with success on german reserve coming up for the fight.	
		11 pm	relieved by No. 3 Coy. M.G. Corps. Company moved back to billets in ALBERT.	[illegible signature]

T2134. Wt. W708—776. 500000. 4/15. Sir J. C. & S.

Army Form C. 2118.

Instructions regarding War Diaries and Intelligence Summaries are contained in F. S. Regs., Part II. and the Staff Manual respectively. Title pages will be prepared in manuscript.

WAR DIARY
or
INTELLIGENCE SUMMARY.
(Erase heading not required.)

Place	Date	Hour	Summary of Events and Information	Remarks and references to Appendices
	JULY		Reference Map 57d S.E.	
S. of SOMME	14		One gun knocked out by shell fire, and deep dug out destroyed burying 4 men (2 died). 4 OR killed 5 OR wounded & 1 OR missing. Very heavy shelling on this day. Gun positions handed over to No 3 Coy :- X 16 b 5.5, X 16 b 8.5, X 17 a 0.1, X 17 c 2.9, X 17 c 3.6, X 16 d 9.2½. These guns for defence of CONTALMAISON. 1 gun at X 16 c 2.1, to defend PEARL WOOD ALLEY. 1 gun X 23 a 3.5 to defend (LOWER WOOD) VALLEY. 1 gun at X 22 b 8.0½ to defend ground behind CONTALMAISON.	
"	15		Quiet day - cleaning men and material. A few shells dropped near ALBERT STN. during night	
"	16		Quiet day - cleaning guns &c. 1. OR to hospital.	
"	17		Quiet day.	
		8.30 pm.	Moved to MAZIE REDOUBT and relieved No 2 Coy. who moved to 'firing line' - bivouac. 1. OR wounded & 1 Officer wounded.	

T2134. Wt. W708-776. 500000. 4/15. Sir J. C. & S.

Army Form C. 2118.

Instructions regarding War Diaries and Intelligence Summaries are contained in F. S. Regs., Part II. and the Staff Manual respectively. Title pages will be prepared in manuscript.

WAR DIARY
or
INTELLIGENCE SUMMARY.
(Erase heading not required.)

Place	Date	Hour	Summary of Events and Information	Remarks and references to Appendices
			Reference Map - Sheet 57d S.E.	
	July			
ALBERT	18		Quiet day. 1 O.R. (died of wounds)	
	19		Normal - inspection of all M. Guns & equipment	
		7 pm.	Company moved to O.B.1. and relieved No 3 Coy M.G. Corps	
			5 O.R. joined from Hospital. 7 O.R. joined from Battn to replace casualties in permanently attached men.	
"	20		Moved to trenches in X27b - quiet day.	
"	21		3 M. Guns moved up under Lt GARDEN and occupied positions in X12a. Heavy shelling by enemy.	
			1 O.R. wounded 6 O.R. joined from Base.	
	22		Very heavy shelling all day. 8 more M. Guns sent up under Capt Law & Lt. LISMORE respectively to report to C.O. 1st Camerons & C.O. 10th Glosters - guns occupied positions in O.G.1 and were at disposal of C.O. Battns	
			11 guns in the line - 3 in defensive positions & 8 at disposal of C.O.s	
			4 O.R. joined from Base.	[signature]

T2134. Wt. W708—776. 500000. 4/15. Sir J. C. & S.

Instructions regarding War Diaries and Intelligence Summaries are contained in F. S. Regs., Part II. and the Staff Manual respectively. Title pages will be prepared in manuscript.

WAR DIARY
or
INTELLIGENCE SUMMARY.
(Erase heading not required.)

Army Form C. 2118.

Place	Date	Hour	Summary of Events and Information	Remarks and references to Appendices
	July		Reference Map – Sheet 57d SE	
	23	12.30 am.	1st D.W. attack on SWITCH LINE. Our M Guns were not required to go forward as the enemy's trenches were not carried. 1 M Gun put out of action by shell fire.	
			3 guns under Lt GARDEN withdrawn to reserve in X.27.b	
			Intense bombardment by enemy at different periods of day.	
			2 O.R. killed & 4 OR wounded.	
	24		Very lively shelling by both sides – no action by M–Guns.	
			Lt H. RIDLER admitted to hospital.	
	25		Company relieved by 70th Bde MG Coy. Moved to billets in BAIZIEUX WOOD arrived 8 pm. with exception of 2 guns which arrived at 3 am 26/7/16.	
	26		Quiet day – Company at inspection.	
			11 OR joined from Base.	
	27		Quiet day. Rifles & guns inspected.	
			No other training by order of 1st D.W.	

T2134. Wt. W708–776. 500000. 4/15. Sir J. C. & S.

Army Form C. 2118.

Instructions regarding War Diaries and Intelligence Summaries are contained in F. S. Regs., Part II. and the Staff Manual respectively. Title pages will be prepared in manuscript.

WAR DIARY
or
INTELLIGENCE SUMMARY.
(Erase heading not required.)

Place	Date	Hour	Summary of Events and Information	Remarks and references to Appendices
	JULY			
BAIZIEUX	28		Commenced training — Morning. Physical drill 9-12 gun drill firing practice.	
"	29		Company training — 1 Section reports to the Battns in Bde each morning for training with Infantry. 1st Bde Sports in afternoon.	
"	30		Physical training in morning	
		11am	Church parade.	
			5. OR joined from Base 1 OR to hospital	
"	31		Company training as before — G.O.C. 1st Div. inspected draft which had arrived since 5/7/16.	
			Capt LAW 1st Cameron Highlanders attached for duty	
			Weather 1-7-16 to 17-7-16. Changeable — a lot of rain	
			18-7-16 " 31-7-16. Fine dry weather.	

1st Brigade.
1st Division.

1st BRIGADE

MACHINE GUN COMPANY

AUGUST 1 9 1 6

1 M G Coy

Army Form C 2118.

Vol 8

Instructions regarding War Diaries and Intelligence Summaries are contained in F.S. Regs., Part II and the Staff Manual respectively. Title Pages will be prepared in manuscript.

WAR DIARY

or

~~INTELLIGENCE SUMMARY~~

(Erase heading not required).

Place.	Date	Hour	Summary of Events and Information.	Remarks and references to Appendices
			WAR DIARY of No. I Machine Gun Company for AUGUST 1916	

Stationery Services Press, X 8. 5,000 7/15

Instructions regarding War Diaries and Intelligence Summaries are contained in F. S. Regs., Part II. and the Staff Manual respectively. Title pages will be prepared in manuscript.

WAR DIARY
or
~~INTELLIGENCE~~ ~~SUMMARY.~~
(Erase heading not required.)

Army Form C. 2118.

Place	Date	Hour	Summary of Events and Information	Remarks and references to Appendices
	1916 Aug			
BAIZIEUX	1		Company training – 1st Bde. was inspected by Corps Commander in afternoon in field N of BAIZIEUX WOOD.	
	2		Company training. Weather fine & sunny.	
	3		Company training. 1st Bde trials for 1st Divn Sports in afternoon	
	4		Company training. 1st Div Sports at MILLENCOURT in afternoon – excellent show. 2 Sgts joined from Base. Pte G. Scott (accidently killed – broke camp at 9 p.m. and was run over by motor lorry at 12 midnight at LA NEUVILLE).	
	5		Company training – 1 OR returned to Base (unfit).	
	6		Church parade. 1 OR (attached) returned to Battn. Fine & sunny	
	7		Company training	
	8		do.	
	9		Company training (field day) Rapid advance in conjunction with Infantry as ammunition supply.	
	10		Wet day. Company lectured on lessons from recent operations. 1 OR to Hospital	
	11		Company ~~etc.~~ training. 1 OR joined from Base.	[signature]

T2134. Wt. W708–776. 500000. 4/15. Sir J. C. & S.

Army Form C. 2118.

WAR DIARY

~~INTELLIGENCE SUMMARY.~~

(*Erase heading not required.*)

Instructions regarding War Diaries and Intelligence Summaries are contained in F. S. Regs., Part II. and the Staff Manual respectively. Title pages will be prepared in manuscript.

Place	Date	Hour	Summary of Events and Information	Remarks and references to Appendices
	1916 Aug			
BAIZIEUX	12		Company training.	
	13		Brigade Church parade. 2nd Lt G.B. Mason attached to Coy from 10th Glosters.	
	14.		Company move to BECOURT 7.15 pm arrived 10 pm. bivouac in field S.W. of BECOURT WOOD . 2 O.R. to Hospital (sick)	
			Lt G.B. Coote to 4th Army Infantry School. Lt J.W. Garden to M.G. Course CAMIERS.	
BECOURT.	15.		Company moved to trenches and relieved No 112 M.G. Coy at 12 noon, and	
S. BAZENTIN-LE-PETIT			occupied positions as follows:- S 2 d 9. 7½, S 2 d ½. 3, S 2 d, 9.6, S 2 d 7.0 S 8 b 8.8, S 8 a 8.7, 2 guns in 'D' Keep, 1 gun in 'C' Keep, 4 guns in 'B' Keep, 1 gun in 'A' Keep, 2 guns in reserve at Coy H.Q. (S1 4 a 2.6)	
			Heavy shelling in afternoon and communication between guns was difficult	
	16.		Enemy continued to shell trenches with all size shells - enemy M.Guns were also very active. 7 of our Machine guns in reserve fired in bursts during the night on points in the neighbourhood of MARTINPUICH and in area M 32 c . An average of 1000 rounds per gun was fired. 2 O.R. wounded	[signature] Lt.

T2134. Wt. W708–776. 500000. 4/15. Sir J. C. & S.

Army Form C. 2118.

Instructions regarding War Diaries and Intelligence Summaries are contained in F. S. Regs., Part II. and the Staff Manual respectively. Title pages will be prepared in manuscript.

WAR DIARY
~~or~~
~~INTELLIGENCE SUMMARY.~~

(Erase heading not required.)

Place	Date	Hour	Summary of Events and Information	Remarks and references to Appendices
S of BAZINTIN LE-PETIT	1916 Aug 17.		Less shelling than yesterday. 'D' Keep heavily shelled in afternoon & 1 Machine Gun damaged. Indirect M.G. fire on area S2d & M32d during the night. This night firing seems to annoy the enemy as he searched for our machine guns with 'pip squeaks'. 1. OR wounded.	
	18.		Very heavy shelling of all localities. 2 guns in front line damaged by shell fire – they were replaced by 2 guns from reserve. Indirect M.G. fire on enemy's trenches and communications vigorously continued. Position of guns now as follows:– S2d ½ 3, S2d 9.2½, S8b 8.8, S2d 9.6, S2d 7.0, S8a 8.7, 1 gun in 'D' Keep, 2 guns in 'C' Keep. 2 guns in 'B' Keep, 1 gun in 'A' Keep 1 gun at Coy H.Q. – 3 damaged. 3 OR Killed, 6 OR wounded.	
	19.	4 a.m.	2 guns under Lieut DUKES were held in readiness to go forward and consolidate part of INTERMEDIATE LINE when captured by BLACK WATCH, but were not required as trench was not taken. Situation lively, heavy shelling of front line by enemy. M.Gun fire on selected points – particularly MARTINPUICH during the night. 4 OR Killed 1 OR to hospital.	[signature]

T2134. Wt. W708–776. 500000. 4/15. Sir J. C. & S.

Army Form C. 2118.

Instructions regarding War Diaries and Intelligence Summaries are contained in F. S. Regs., Part II. and the Staff Manual respectively. Title pages will be prepared in manuscript.

WAR DIARY

~~or~~

~~INTELLIGENCE SUMMARY.~~

(Erase heading not required.)

Place	Date	Hour	Summary of Events and Information	Remarks and references to Appendices
S of BAZINTIN LE-PETIT	1916 Aug. 20.		Quieter day. No I Coy was relieved by No III Coy at 9 a.m. Company then moved into support in trenches in MAMETZ WOOD and bivouaced in trench & wood - bottom Western edge. H.Q. at X 24 c 5.4.	
		6 pm 6.30 pm	a large number of heavy shells fell just clear of W edge of MAMETZ WOOD about X 23 d. 1 O.R. missing 1. OR wounded.	
	21.		As Company area was heavily shelled we moved to dugouts & bivouacs X 24 a with HQs at X 24 a 2.4. Guns & equipment cleaned.	
	22.		Quiet day - Machine guns & ammunition belts inspected.	
	23.		Quiet day - Company refitted for action as far as possible. 1 O.R. wounded, 2 OR joined from base.	
	24.		Normal, the company worked on improving present dug outs & building new 'splinter proofs'. Lt. J. LISMORE to Hospital (sick).	
	25.		Quiet day, continued work on 'splinter proofs'. Officers went to trenches to select special positions for firing on HIGH WOOD from 15th Div. area - the intention being to keep down all observation from HIGH WOOD prior to attack by 1st Bde	[illegible]

T2134. Wt. W708—776. 500000. 4/15. Sir J. C. & S.

Army Form C. 2118.

Instructions regarding War Diaries and Intelligence Summaries are contained in F. S. Regs., Part II. and the Staff Manual respectively. Title pages will be prepared in manuscript.

WAR DIARY

~~or INTELLIGENCE SUMMARY.~~

(Erase heading not required.)

Place	Date	Hour	Summary of Events and Information	Remarks and references to Appendices
MAMETZ WOOD	1916 Aug 26.		Some shelling of MAMETZ WOOD in afternoon. Preparation for trenches. Heavy rain in evening. 8 OR joined from base. Special parties were working on the positions selected in 15th Div area – emplacements are being dug in saps off main trenches.	
	27.		No I Coy relieved No 19 MG Coy in HIGH WOOD area at 7 am. Relief complete by 9 am. Coy HQr BAZENTIN-LE-GRAND (S15b 1½.6). Some rain fell during the day. 1 OR joined from base.	
BAZENTIN-LE-GRAND			Gun positions occupied as follows:–	
			3 guns in HIGH WOOD. 1 gun in SAP 1, 1 " " SAP 3, 1 " " SAP 5	
			3 guns in SEAFORTH TRENCH. S4 d ½.3, S4 c 9½.3½, S4 c 9.4.	
			3 guns in buildings BAZENTIN-LE-GRAND	
			7 guns in trench S15 a & b (6 of these guns are detailed for special work under Lt Mackenzie.	
			Heavy shelling of SEAFORTH TRENCH during the evening. 1 OR joined from Base	[signature]

T2134. Wt. W708—776. 500000. 4/15. Sir J. C. & S.

Army Form C 2118.

Instructions regarding War Diaries and Intelligence Summaries are contained in F.S. Regs., Part II and the Staff Manual respectively. Title Pages will be prepared in manuscript.

WAR DIARY
or
~~INTELLIGENCE SUMMARY~~
(Erase heading not required).

Place.	Date	Hour	Summary of Events and Information.	Remarks and references to Appendices
BAZINTIN-LE-GRAND	1916 Aug 28		Dull weather - Heavy rain in morning. Trenches in very bad condition owing to rain	
		2 am	Heavy barrage by enemy's guns in Support line.	
			Indirect Machine Gun fire on tracks & roads behind the enemy's line all night.	
			M.G. fire also directed during the day on MARTINPUICH cross roads M34 d 8.4	
			Special emplacements in 15th Div. area for Divisional operations now complete	
			1 OR. wounded 1 OR to Hospital	
	29		Heavy rain - trenches full of water	
	28		Lt. J. A. Royds appointed 2nd in Command of No. 8 M.G. Coy.	
			Lt. L.W. Garden do No. 33 M.G. Coy.	
			2nd Lt. E.W. Doig joined from Base	
			2nd Lt. N.R. Gorringe do.	
			The above Officers are struck off strength from this date.	
	29	1.30 AM.	A strong enemy patrol approached SAP. 5 (HIGH WOOD) and threw bombs - our Machine Gun in this sap opened fire on them & drove enemy back with many casualties.	[signature]

Army Form C 2118.

WAR DIARY

~~or~~

~~INTELLIGENCE~~ SUMMARY

(Erase heading not required).

Instructions regarding War Diaries and Intelligence Summaries are contained in F.S. Regs., Part II and the Staff Manual respectively. Title Pages will be prepared in manuscript.

Place.	Date	Hour	Summary of Events and Information.	Remarks and references to Appendices
BAZENTIN-LE-GRAND	1916 Aug. 29.		Four guns fired from trench S 15 c & d on areas M 33 c & d and M 34 c & d. Support reserve & communication trenches heavily shelled during night.	
	30.		Usual heavy shelling – weather very bad	
		1.43 am	After heavy shelling the enemy attempted to raid our trenches in the vicinity of SAP 5 – our Machine Guns opened rapid fire and party were driven back. About 7 belts of 250 rounds were fired & some casualties were caused to enemy.	
			6 guns were moved to selected positions in the 5th Divn area to E/r of HIGH WOOD to participate in 'sham' smoke attack – which was however cancelled & guns were withdrawn.	
			Trench running through S 15 a & b behind BAZENTIN-LE-GRAND was heavily shelled during night – probably because indirect M.G. fire from this trench had annoyed the enemy	
			2 OR joined from Base. 1 OR to hospital (sick) 1 OR wounded & 1 OR missing	[signature] Lt.

Stationery Services Press, X 8. 5,000 7/15

Instructions regarding War Diaries and Intelligence Summaries are contained in F.S. Regs., Part II and the Staff Manual respectively. Title Pages will be prepared in manuscript.

WAR DIARY
or
~~INTELLIGENCE SUMMARY~~
(Erase heading not required).

Army Form C 2118.

Place.	Date	Hour	Summary of Events and Information.	Remarks and references to Appendices
BAZINTIN LE-GRAND	1916 Aug 31.		From early morning the enemy shelled HIGH WOOD and BAZINTIN-LE GRAND heavily.	
MAMETZ WOOD			No I M.G. Coy was relieved by No. 2 M.G. Coy and moved into support area in MAMETZ WOOD – relief complete by 11 a.m.	
			Weather much brighter.	
			A large number of 'gas shells' were fired into MAMETZ WOOD during the night – a few men in the Company were slightly gassed.	
			3 O.R. killed & 1 O.R. wounded.	
				[illegible signature]

Stationery Services Press, X 8. 5,000 7/15

1st Brigade.

1st Division.

1st MACHINE GUN COMPANY ::: SEPTEMBER 1916.

Army Form C. 2118.

Instructions regarding War Diaries and Intelligence Summaries are contained in F. S. Regs., Part II. and the Staff Manual respectively. Title Pages will be prepared in manuscript.

WAR DIARY
or
INTELLIGENCE SUMMARY

(Erase heading not required.)

Vol 9

Place	Date	Hour	Summary of Events and Information	Remarks and references to Appendices
			War Diary of No 1 Machine Gun Company for September 1916	

2449 Wt. W14957/M90 750,000 1/16 J.B.C. & A. Forms/C.2118/12.

Army Form C. 2118.

Instructions regarding War Diaries and Intelligence Summaries are contained in F. S. Regs., Part II. and the Staff Manual respectively. Title Pages will be prepared in manuscript.

WAR DIARY
or
~~INTELLIGENCE SUMMARY~~
(Erase heading not required.)

Place	Date	Hour	Summary of Events and Information	Remarks and references to Appendices
	Sept. 1916			
	1		Company training	
			1 O.R. Wounded	
	2		Paraded at 7 a.m. and moved up to trenches. Relieved No. 2 Coy. in HIGH WOOD Sector and occupied M.G. positions as under with Coy. H.Q. at S 15 6. 1½ 6. BAZENTIN le GRAND.	
			3 guns in HIGH WOOD — 1 gun in Sap. 1; 1 " " " 2; 1 " " " 5	
			3 guns in SEAFORTH ALLEY — 1 gun S 4 d ½. 3; 1 " S 4 c 9½, 3½; 1 " S 4 c 9 4	
			2 guns in buildings in BAZENTIN le GRAND	
			2 guns in trench S 15 a 2.6.	
			6 guns in 15th Div. area	

2449 Wt. W14957/M90 750,000 1/16 J.B.C. & A. Forms/C.2118/12.

Army Form C. 2118.

Instructions regarding War Diaries and Intelligence Summaries are contained in F. S. Regs., Part II. and the Staff Manual respectively. Title Pages will be prepared in manuscript.

WAR DIARY
or
~~INTELLIGENCE SUMMARY~~

(Erase heading not required.)

Place	Date	Hour	Summary of Events and Information	Remarks and references to Appendices
	Sept. 1916			
	2		During sham smoke attacks by 15th. Div. at 2 p.m. 4 guns fired from selected positions on HIGH WOOD and traversed from there to left – 6000 r fired.	
			Fairly heavy retaliation.	
			During night heavy M.G. fire on points behind HIGH WOOD.	
			H.Q. moved to advanced Bde. H.Q. in BAZENTIN le GRAND.	
			1 O.R. wounded	
	3		Attack by 1st. Bde.	
			The guns of the Company were detailed to co-operate in the attack as follows;	
			Right Section — 3 guns under Capt. Law to work with the Cameron Highlanders.	
			Left Section — 3 guns under Lieut. Mason to work with Black Watch.	
			Special Section — 6 guns under Lieut. McKenzie to bring flanking fire on to HIGH WOOD.	
			Reserve Section — 4 guns under Lieut. Doig to carry out overhead fire.	

2449 Wt. W14957/M90 750,000 1/16 J.B.C. & A. Forms/C.2118/12.

Army Form C. 2118.

Instructions regarding War Diaries and Intelligence Summaries are contained in F. S. Regs., Part II. and the Staff Manual respectively. Title Pages will be prepared in manuscript.

WAR DIARY
or
~~INTELLIGENCE SUMMARY~~

(Erase heading not required.)

Place	Date	Hour	Summary of Events and Information	Remarks and references to Appendices
	Sept. 1916 3		Detailed reports :-	
			Right Section 3 guns under Capt. Law.	
			2 guns were placed in position in SEAFORTH TRENCH. These guns were to hold our line when vacated by attacking troops.	
			1 gun was dismounted in the front trench in readiness to go over with the consolidating platoons of D. Coy	
			The gun went forward with the platoon	
			On the way over, 2 of the team were killed and 2 wounded, however the gun was got up into position on the right of C. Coy. the Camerons. The trench was very much knocked about at this point so the gun went forward to a shell hole some 20 yds. in front of the line taken up by the Camerons.	
			The gun opened fire at a group of Germans who could be seen at times about the Crest line.	
			The counter attack was made with troops from 3 directions viz.- from N.E. corner of HIGH WOOD, from DELVILLE WOOD and from the trees in M. 30c and M. 36a. The gun at once opened fire on these latter. They then became aware that the enemy had managed to advance on the left and that were coming back and leaving the flank open.	

2449 Wt. W14957/M90 750,000 1/16 J.B.C. & A. Forms/C.2118/12.

Army Form C. 2118.

Instructions regarding War Diaries and Intelligence Summaries are contained in F. S. Regs., Part II. and the Staff Manual respectively. Title Pages will be prepared in manuscript.

WAR DIARY

or

~~INTELLIGENCE SUMMARY~~

(Erase heading not required.)

Place	Date	Hour	Summary of Events and Information	Remarks and references to Appendices
	Sept. 1916 3		Rifle fire opened from the left at the gun team so the gun was brought back to keep in line with the infantry. They claim to have inflicted over 100 casualties on the enemy. The enemy advanced in small bodies. They were all armed with rifles and bayonets and were wearing soft caps. Left Section: 3 guns under Lieut. Mason One gun in Sap 1 to be sent over to take up a position in or near the crater. One gun in Sap 3 and one gun in Sap 5 to remain in position when the assaulting troops vacated the trench. At Zero the mine was blown up and the Right Company of the Black Watch went forward. Lieut. Mason was standing by with his gun when the gun was struck with shrapnel. Lieut Mason then went to Sap 3 and brought up the gun there. About 12-30 P.m. the crater party went over and Lieut. Mason took his team with them. The gun got into the crater but Lieut Mason decided that the gun would be better placed if pushed forward so he took the gun 50 yds. up along the edge of the wood and started to dig himself in on a line with the left of the Camerons.	

2449 Wt. W14957/M90 750,000 1/16 J.B.C. & A. Forms/C.2118/12.

Army Form C. 2118.

Instructions regarding War Diaries and Intelligence Summaries are contained in F. S. Regs., Part II. and the Staff Manual respectively. Title Pages will be prepared in manuscript.

WAR DIARY
or
~~INTELLIGENCE SUMMARY~~
(Erase heading not required.)

Place	Date	Hour	Summary of Events and Information	Remarks and references to Appendices
	Sept 1916 3		The counter attack then came. Strong parties of Germans were advancing down the road running half right from S.E. corner of the WOOD and others could be seen coming over the ridge to attack the Camerons further to the right. They were wearing soft caps and were fully equipped with rifles and bayonets. Fire was opened on the parties on the road and many casualties were caused. The gun then got a broken muzzle cup and was out of action. Lieut. Mason at once sent back for his third gun. While waiting for it, a party of Germans armed with bombs attacked the crater from the left of the WOOD and the Machine Gun was taken back to the crater. Here the team found only dead and wounded and the Lewis guns out of action. Lieut. Mason was wounded in the CRATER as the team ran back to our own front line. Strength of team 1 officer 7 O.R. Casualties 1 O.R. killed 1 officer } 5 O.R. } Wounded.	

2449 Wt. W14957/M90 750,000 1/16 J.B.C. & A. Forms/C.2118/12.

Army Form C. 2118.

Instructions regarding War Diaries and Intelligence Summaries are contained in F. S. Regs., Part II. and the Staff Manual respectively. Title Pages will be prepared in manuscript.

WAR DIARY
or
~~INTELLIGENCE SUMMARY~~

(Erase heading not required.)

Place	Date	Hour	Summary of Events and Information	Remarks and references to Appendices
	Sept 1916 3		Special Section under Lieut McKenzie These guns were placed in position in the 15th Div. area to bring flanking fire to bear on HIGH WOOD from the left. From 1 hr. 40 min. before Zero the guns fired on HIGH WOOD in bursts. About Zero the mine was blown up and the R.E. appliances brought into action. All 6 guns at once opened intense fire on HIGH WOOD. The smoke in the wood was too thick for any observation but as the Germans undoubtedly left their trench heavy casualties must have been inflicted. Immediately after Zero batches of Germans were seen leaving HIGH WOOD and bolting over the CREST. The two front guns caught each party and they claim 60 to 70 casualties. There is no doubt on this point. During the counter attack nothing could be seen of Germans advancing but heavy shelling by the enemy was opened on our trenches. Slow bursts of fire were maintained until dusk. 24000 r fired Casualties, 2 O.R. wounded.	

2449 Wt. W14957/M90 750,000 1/16 J.B.C. & A. Forms/C.2118/12.

Army Form C. 2118.

Instructions regarding War Diaries and Intelligence Summaries are contained in F. S. Regs., Part II. and the Staff Manual respectively. Title Pages will be prepared in manuscript.

WAR DIARY
or
~~INTELLIGENCE SUMMARY~~
(Erase heading not required.)

Place	Date	Hour	Summary of Events and Information	Remarks and references to Appendices
	Sept 1916 3		Reserve Section under Lieut. Doig – 4 guns These guns were placed in position in BAZENTIN le GRAND They were ordered to fire during the night 2/3 Sept. on the ground immediately in front of the SWITCH LINE from HIGH WOOD to the RIGHT of the ground held by the Camerons. Fire was to open again 2 hours before Zero and continue till one hour after Zero. This was carried out. The guns fired in bursts during the night. They opened again at 10 a.m. firing in bursts increasing to intense 5 minutes before Zero until 6 minutes after Zero. They ceased fire at 1 P.m. At 3-30 P.m. the Germans counter-attacks began and the guns opened fire at once and continued firing until 6 p.m. in heavy bursts. During the day 40,000 r were fired by these guns. It is impossible to state what casualties were inflicted on the enemy but as very heavy fire was maintained over a large extent of ground casualties must have been considerable.	

2449 Wt. W14957/M90 750,000 1/16 J.B.C. & A. Forms/C.2118/12.

Army Form C. 2118.

WAR DIARY
or
~~INTELLIGENCE SUMMARY~~

(Erase heading not required.)

Instructions regarding War Diaries and Intelligence Summaries are contained in F. S. Regs., Part II. and the Staff Manual respectively. Title Pages will be prepared in manuscript.

Place	Date	Hour	Summary of Events and Information	Remarks and references to Appendices
	Sept. 1916			
	3		The section had no casualties.	
	4		No action. Intermittent shelling of our trenches.	
	5		Company relieved by No. 3 Coy. and proceed to Maxse redoubt near BEACOURT WOOD.	
	6		Company Training	
			6 O.R. joined from base	
			2 O.R. killed	
			10 O.R. wounded	
			3 O.R. missing	
			4 O.R. sick to hospital	
	7		Company Training	
	8		Company Training	
			1 O.R. rejoined from hospital	
	9		Company Training	
	10		Company moved into billets at MILLENCOURT.	
			1 O.R. rejoined from hospital.	
	11		Company moved into billets at LA HUSSOYE.	

2449 Wt. W14957/M90 750,000 1/16 J.B.C. & A. Forms/C.2118/12.

Army Form C. 2118.

Instructions regarding War Diaries and Intelligence Summaries are contained in F. S. Regs., Part II. and the Staff Manual respectively. Title Pages will be prepared in manuscript.

WAR DIARY
or
~~INTELLIGENCE SUMMARY~~
(Erase heading not required.)

Place	Date	Hour	Summary of Events and Information	Remarks and references to Appendices
	Sept. 1916			
	12		Company Training	
			4 O.R. joined from 1st Black Watch	
	13		Company Training	
			Lieut Lismore sick to England	
			1 O.R. evacuated sick	
			Honours – Military Medal	
			No. 20370 Sergt. Redpath N. (since deceased), No. 20410 Cpl. Bernard J.	
	14		Company Training	
	15		Company Training	
			Lt. MURLEY returned to England to command a service company	
	16		Company moved to Billets at BRESLE	
			Lt. J. S. SNOWBALL reported and took over the duties of 2nd in command.	
			6 O.R. joined from Black Watch	
	17		Church Parades	

2449 Wt. W14957/M90 750,000 1/16 J.B.C. & A. Forms/C.2118/12.

Army Form C. 2118.

Instructions regarding War Diaries and Intelligence Summaries are contained in F. S. Regs., Part II. and the Staff Manual respectively. Title Pages will be prepared in manuscript.

WAR DIARY
or
~~INTELLIGENCE SUMMARY~~
(Erase heading not required.)

Place	Date	Hour	Summary of Events and Information	Remarks and references to Appendices
	Sept. 1916			
	18		Company moved up to BECOURT WOOD via LAVIEVILLE, ALBERT. Night in dugouts, shelters etc.	
			4 O.R. joined from 10th Glosters.	
			7 O.R. joined from Base Depot	
	19		Relieved 140th Coy. with 4 guns and 141st Coy with 6 guns	
			Positions of guns:-	
			COUGH DROP line M 35 a 5.4 } Lieut. Doig	
			do M 35 b 5 3 }	
			STAR FISH line M 35 c 6 4 }	
			do M 35 c 9.3 }	
			HIGH WOOD line S 4 b 5.6 } Lieut. Flux	
			do S 4 b. 8.5 }	
			do S 4.a. 2.9 }	
			do S 4.a. 4.8. }	
			It was also intended to send 4 guns into DROP ALLEY but the Germans bombed into this trench about 8 P.m. just before the relief so these 4 guns were ordered to stand by at our H.Q.	

2449 Wt. W14957/M90 750,000 1/16 J.B.C. & A. Forms/C.2118/12.

Army Form C. 2118.

Instructions regarding War Diaries and Intelligence Summaries are contained in F. S. Regs., Part II. and the Staff Manual respectively. Title Pages will be prepared in manuscript.

WAR DIARY
or
~~INTELLIGENCE SUMMARY~~

(Erase heading not required.)

Place	Date	Hour	Summary of Events and Information	Remarks and references to Appendices
	Sept 1916 19th		Position of our H.Q. BAZENTIN Le GRAND. 3.15 b.0.5	
	20th		Two more guns were sent up under Lieut Mackenzie. A successful attack was made on DROP ALLEY at night so that one of our guns was moved there. Position of guns now was (a) DROP ALLEY. M 35 a 7.7. (b) COUGH DROP M 35 a 6.2. (c) Do Do M 35 a 5.2. (d) Sap M 35 c 4.8. } Lieut Dorg; (e) STARFISH Line M 35 a 7.3. (f) Do M 35 a 4.6. } Lieut Mackenzie.	
			The four guns in HIGH WOOD line remained in the same positions. The remaining 6 guns of the Company in Dug-outs at BAZENTIN Le GRAND. During ~~their~~ attack the STARFISH was bombarded heavilly by Artillery and Trench Mortars but quietened down later. 2 O.R. wounded	
	21st		Indirect fire was carried out by M.M.G Battery attached to us on road running through M 22 d and M 28 b.	
			SIX guns of No 3 Company were attached to us and went up into the FLERS LINE. Position of our 10 guns in the line (a) DROPALLEY M 29 d 2.1. (b) Do M 35 a 7.7. (c) COUGH DROP M 35 a 6.5. (d) SAP M 35 c 4.8. (e) STARFISH LINE M 35 c 4.5. f Do M 35 c 7.3. 15 } Lieut Coote	

2449 Wt. W14957/M90 750,000 1/16 J.B.C. & A. Forms/C.2118/12.

Instructions regarding War Diaries and Intelligence Summaries are contained in F. S. Regs., Part II. and the Staff Manual respectively. Title Pages will be prepared in manuscript.

WAR DIARY
or
~~INTELLIGENCE SUMMARY~~
(Erase heading not required.)

Army Form C. 2118.

Place	Date	Hour	Summary of Events and Information	Remarks and references to Appendices
	Sept 1916 21st	T	The four guns in the HIGH WOOD line remained the same Heavy shelling by enemy Artillery 1 OR Killed. 3 OR wounded. 2 OR. Sick Hospital.	
	22nd		An advanced trench was dug about the SUNKEN ROAD in front of DROPALLEY running down through M 28 d 9 0 M 29 c 9 0. Digging parties found by 6th Welch + 10th Gloucesters. Three of our guns were detailed to go out with the digging parties to man this trench.	
			At 10.45 p.m. the two guns from STARFISH Line were taken up to DROP ALLEY. The digging party was then out. The gun from M29 d 0.6 went out under Lieut Coote and Sgt Bradley and dug in in a shell hole on the farther side of the SUNKEN ROAD. The gun for M 22 c 6.0 went out under 2Lt Mackenzie and dug in in a shell hole behind the SUNKEN ROAD. Lt Mackenzie returned to HQ	
			2Lt Bailey took up a gun to about M 29 c 0.0 and it dug in in a Shell Hole. Digging Party not molested.	
			Position of the guns	
			(d) DROPALLEY M 29 d 2.1.	
			(e) (f) (g) } COUGH DROP.	
			(h) STARFISH Line M 35 c 4.5.	
			(j) Do M 35 b 7.0.	
			(k) Do M 35 b 6.0	

2449 Wt. W14957/M90 750,000 1/16 J.B.C. & A. Forms/C.2118/12.

Instructions regarding War Diaries and Intelligence Summaries are contained in F. S. Regs., Part II. and the Staff Manual respectively. Title Pages will be prepared in manuscript.

WAR DIARY
or
~~INTELLIGENCE SUMMARY~~
(Erase heading not required.)

Army Form C. 2118.

Place	Date	Hour	Summary of Events and Information	Remarks and references to Appendices
	Sept 1916 22nd		Indirect fire was carried out on roads running through M22d & M28b	
			A German Machine Gun of the latest (1916) pattern was recovered by Lt Coote	
			2Lieut Gorringe to Hospital (SICK)	
			2Lieut RL Bailey joined the Company.	
	23rd		Our 10 guns relieved by No 3 Coy Company moved to bivouacs in MAMETZ WOOD Lt Doig remained behind attached to No 3 Coy to do indirect fire. During the four days in the trenches we recovered 3 Vickers Guns.	
	24th		Company Cleaned guns etc	
	25th		Lt Coote relieved LT Doig 2 sections under LT's Mackenzie, Bailey & Flux stood to from 2 pm to move up to protect the rear of the Cavalry if they should break through.	
	26th		Lieut Coote and section returned to the Company 3 OR to Hospital (Sick).	
	27th		Company relieved by 141st Company & moved at 8 pm to BRESLE Via BOTTOMWOOD, LOZENGE WOOD, and ALBERT. arrived about 12.30AM	

2449 Wt. W14957/M90 750,000 1/16 J.B.C. & A. Forms/C.2118/12.

Instructions regarding War Diaries and Intelligence Summaries are contained in F. S. Regs., Part II. and the Staff Manual respectively. Title Pages will be prepared in manuscript.

WAR DIARY
or
~~INTELLIGENCE SUMMARY~~

(Erase heading not required.)

Army Form C. 2118.

Place	Date	Hour	Summary of Events and Information	Remarks and references to Appendices
	SEPT 28th 1916		Company cleaning up	
	29th		Company cleaning guns &c Lieut Coote to Hospital (Sick)	
	30th		Company Training Lieut Coote rejoined	

J. S. Snowball
Lieut & Adjt
No 1 Machine Gun Coy

2449 Wt. W14957/M90 750,000 1/16 J.B.C. & A. Forms/C.2118/12.

1st Brigade.

1st Division

1st MACHINE GUN COMPANY ::: OCTOBER 1916.

Instructions regarding War Diaries and Intelligence Summaries are contained in F. S. Regs., Part II. and the Staff Manual respectively. Title Pages will be prepared in manuscript.

WAR DIARY
or
~~INTELLIGENCE SUMMARY~~

(Erase heading not required.)

No. I Machine Gun Company

Army Form C. 2118.

Vol 10

Place	Date 1916	Hour	Summary of Events and Information	Remarks and references to Appendices
BRASLE	Oct. 1		Reverted to Winter time, Sunday.	
JS	2		Transport left for ABBEVILLE area at 5-30 am. also billeting party under Lieut Coote.	
JS	3		Company paraded for move to new area at 6 am. Embussed on AMIENS-ALBERT Road at 8 am. Route via AMIENS and ABBEVILLE arrived FRIREULLES at 4 pm. Men billeted at FRIREULLES, officers & H.Q. at Château HYMMEVILLE.	
JS	4		Cleaning billets &c. Lt. Snowball in command of Company. Major Angell, Lt. Coote, 2Lt. Dukes on leave to U.K. from 6/10/16. 2 O.R. to Hospital	
JS	5		Company training Honours & Awards 20373 Sgt. Fraser H. 20436 " Kurtshner J. 20370 " Redpath W. 20453 " Jones A.L. 22172 Pte. Lindsay J. } Awarded Military Medal London Gazette dated 12-9-16	
JS	6		Company Training	

2449 Wt. W14957/M90 750,000 1/16 J.B.C. & A. Forms/C.2118/12.

Instructions regarding War Diaries and Intelligence Summaries are contained in F. S. Regs., Part II. and the Staff Manual respectively. Title Pages will be prepared in manuscript.

WAR DIARY
or
~~INTELLIGENCE SUMMARY~~

(Erase heading not required.)

No. I Machine Gun Company

Army Form C. 2118.

Place	Date	Hour	Summary of Events and Information	Remarks and references to Appendices
FRIREULLES	1916 Oct. 7		Company training. Company (including Transport) inspected by C.O. 2 O.R. sick to hospital.	
do	8		Church Parades.	
do	9		Company training	
do	10		Company training	
do	11		Company training	
do	12		Company training	
do	13		Company training	
do	14		Company training	
			2/Lt. R.L. Bailey on leave to U.K. from 16/10/16.	
do	15		Church Parades	
			2Lt. G.H. Lister M.G.C. reported.	
do	16		Company training	
do	17		Company training	
do	18		Company training. Major Angell resumed command of Company.	
			Major Angell, Lt. Coote, 2Lt. Dukes returned from leave	
do	19		Company training	

2449 Wt. W14957/M90 750,000 1/16 J.B.C. & A. Forms/C.2118/12.

Instructions regarding War Diaries and Intelligence Summaries are contained in F. S. Regs., Part II. and the Staff Manual respectively. Title Pages will be prepared in manuscript.

WAR DIARY

or

~~INTELLIGENCE SUMMARY~~

(Erase heading not required.)

No. I Machine Gun Company

Army Form C. 2118.

Place	Date	Hour	Summary of Events and Information	Remarks and references to Appendices
FRIREULLES	1916 Oct. 20		Brigade Route March. QUESNOY - ARREST - FRANLEU - CHAMPAGNE	
	21		Company training	
JH	22		Church Parades. Brigade mounted GYMKHANA at MIANNAY	
JH	23		Company training	
JH	24		Company training	
JH	25		Company training	
JH	26		Company training	
JH	27		Division Route March FRANLEU - MIANNAY - TREPORT main road - OCHANCOURT - FRANLEU	
JH	28		Company training. Company inspected by Major - Genl. E. P. Strickland C.M.G., DSO, commanding 1st Division 2Lt Bailey rejoined from leave	
JH	29		Church Parades. Transport left for new area	
JH	30		Company training	
JH	31		Company moved by Bus via AMIENS to HENENCOURT. Billeted in HENENCOURT WOOD.	

J. S. Snowball
Lieut & Adjt
No 1 Machine Gun Coy.

2449 Wt. W14957/M90 750,000 1/16 J.B.C. & A. Forms/C.2118/12.

1st Brigade.

1st Division.

<u>1st MACHINE GUN COMPANY ::: NOVEMBER 1916</u>.

Army Form C. 2118.

WAR DIARY

No 1 COMPANY ~~or~~ MACHINE GUN CORPS.

~~INTELLIGENCE SUMMARY~~

(Erase heading not required.)

Instructions regarding War Diaries and Intelligence Summaries are contained in F. S. Regs., Part II. and the Staff Manual respectively. Title Pages will be prepared in manuscript.

Vol XI

Place	Date	Hour	Summary of Events and Information	Remarks and references to Appendices
HENENCOURT	1/11/16		Company Training	
"	2/11/16		" "	
"	3/11/16		" " 3 O.R. evacuated (sick) to hospital	
"	4/11/16		" "	
"	5/11/16		Company marched to new area (BECOURT HILL CAMP) via ALBERT. Lieut B. Coote left to join No 25. M.G. Coy.	
BECOURT	6/11/16		Company Training	
"	7/11/16		" " 100 MEN on Brigade fatigue	
"	8/11/16		" " 2 Sections on " "	
"	9/11/16		" " " " "	
"	10/11/16		" " " " "	
"	11/11/16		" " " " " 2/Lieut. P. J. Flux evacuated to hospital ~~[illegible]~~ wounded	
"	12/11/16		Church Parades 2 Sections on Brigade fatigue 2/Lieut Doig evacuated (sick) to hospital	
"	13/11/16		Company Training " " " " 3 O.R. joined from Base.	
"	12/11/16		Lieut J S Arrowball left for short leave to U.K.	
"	14/11/16		Company Training 2 Sections on Brigade fatigue	
"	15/11/16		" " no fatigue. Major Angell 2/Lieut Dukes, 2/Lieut Bailey & 4 O.R. evacuated to Isolation hospital, No 2 Field Ambulance Millencourt. Lieut Atkinson joined from Base Depot	

2449 Wt. W14957/M90 750,000 1/16 J.B.C. & A. Forms/C.2118/12.

Army Form C. 2118.

Instructions regarding War Diaries and Intelligence Summaries are contained in F. S. Regs., Part II. and the Staff Manual respectively. Title Pages will be prepared in manuscript.

WAR DIARY

No1 COMPANY or MACHINE GUN CORPS ~~INTELLIGENCE SUMMARY~~

(Erase heading not required.)

Place	Date	Hour	Summary of Events and Information	Remarks and references to Appendices
	16/11/16		Company left Becourt area & moved up to High Wood area; being billeted in bivouacs opposite the brewery - Bazentin-le-grand. The night 16th & 17th very cold & hard frost.	
			2/Lieut Boyle joined from Base Depot	
	17/11/16		Four guns ammunition and limber sent to Gullancourt to report to Major Angell.	
			Rations for men evacuated to Millencourt sent by limber 6 A.M.	
			The Company is now so depleted that it is impossible to run it as four sections. It is therefore divided into two complete sections A & B and the remainder are called Headquarters	
			Divisional order one complete section to be kept for use of 3rd Brigade. Company Sergeant Major Souter and A. Section told off for this	
			Orders received for B Section to take over from 150th M.G. COY on night 17th to 18th	
			Relief arranged & trenches inspected by myself, 2/Lieut Boyle & 6 guides	
			It was decided not to occupy the front line positions, but to keep two guns in close support, & two in reserve	
			Positions of support guns No1:- M.17 D.5.3. Abbaye trench	
			No2:- M.17 D.6.5. Snag support	
			" " reserve guns No1:- M.29 b.1.3. Flers support	
			" " " " No2:- M.29 b.2.3. " "	
			2/Lieut Boyle now being absent Sgt Jones remained in Command of this Section	

Instructions regarding War Diaries and Intelligence Summaries are contained in F. S. Regs., Part II. and the Staff Manual respectively. Title Pages will be prepared in manuscript.

WAR DIARY

No 1 COMPANY MACHINE GUN CORPS

or

~~INTELLIGENCE SUMMARY~~

(Erase heading not required.)

Army Form C. 2118.

Place	Date	Hour	Summary of Events and Information	Remarks and references to Appendices
			[illegible] carried to [illegible] Wood [illegible] Park	
	17/11/16		B Section marched off 4 a.m. guns [illegible] [illegible] [illegible] [illegible] met at	
			[illegible] [illegible] [illegible] [illegible] [illegible] [illegible] [illegible] [illegible] [illegible]	
			[illegible] [illegible]. ~~[illegible]~~ 2 section [illegible] – the [illegible] guns [illegible] [illegible] [illegible]	
			The [illegible] guns [illegible] [illegible] [illegible] [illegible] complete 8 a.m.	
			[illegible] [illegible] [illegible] [illegible] [illegible] [illegible] [illegible] to 3rd Brigade and	
	18/11/16		A Section under C.S.M. moved back [illegible] [illegible] [illegible] [illegible]	
			They were to be rationed [illegible] [illegible] [illegible] 29th	
			[illegible] [illegible] [illegible] [illegible] [illegible] [illegible] [illegible] [illegible] 5 p.m.	
			Headquarters comprising all the remainder [illegible] [illegible] [illegible] [illegible] Park [illegible] [illegible] Wood	
			[illegible] for Headquarters and B Section taken [illegible] [illegible] [illegible] [illegible] [illegible]	
			[illegible], [illegible] [illegible] – 5 p.m. – to [illegible] [illegible]. [illegible] [illegible] [illegible] [illegible]	
			[illegible]	
			[illegible] from [illegible] [illegible] [illegible] [illegible] [illegible] [illegible] all [illegible]	
			[illegible] [illegible] 16th – 17th [illegible] [illegible] [illegible] [illegible] [illegible] [illegible], [illegible]	
			[illegible] [illegible] [illegible] [illegible] [illegible] [illegible] [illegible] [illegible]	
			[illegible] [illegible] for [illegible] [illegible]	
	19/11/16		[illegible] [illegible] [illegible] all [illegible]. Headquarters [illegible] [illegible] at M.17b.2.3.	
			No Casualties	
			Two new emplacements dug at M.17b.1.3. and 2.3. [illegible] [illegible] [illegible] [illegible]	
			[illegible] cleared and [illegible] boarded	
			3 p.m. [illegible] [illegible] of B. Section. [illegible] [illegible] [illegible] [illegible] [illegible]	
			[illegible] guns [illegible] [illegible] overhead fire [illegible] [illegible] [illegible].	
			[illegible] [illegible]	
			Weather fair	
			[illegible] [illegible] [illegible] [illegible] to [illegible] Headquarters.	

2449 Wt. W14957/M90 750,000 1/16 J.B.C. & A. Forms/C.2118/12.

Instructions regarding War Diaries and Intelligence Summaries are contained in F. S. Regs., Part II. and the Staff Manual respectively. Title Pages will be prepared in manuscript.

WAR DIARY

No 1 COMPANY or MACHINE GUN CORPS

~~INTELLIGENCE SUMMARY~~

(Erase heading not required.)

Army Form C. 2118.

Place	Date	Hour	Summary of Events and Information	Remarks and references to Appendices
	20/11/16		Sergeant Lamond reports heavy shelling of support line. Enemy [illegible] 50 yards distance and [illegible]. Aeroplane [illegible] during day. Headquarters shelled [illegible] 4.2's and Private Dale wounded in line. Weather very fair. [illegible]	
	21/11/16		[illegible] Company [illegible] Corporal [illegible] took over from Sergeant Lamond. German aeroplane very low over our line, fired at [illegible] marked [illegible] British [illegible], and no [illegible]. [illegible] in evening.	
	22/11/16		First Brigade relieved by 2nd Brigade. O.C. No 2 M.G. COY would not arrange to see me re relief, preferring to place his guns where he liked & when he liked. He gave me permission however to evacuate guns after 7 A.M. Headquarters moved off at 5-30 A.M. B. Section to catch 7-30 pm train if possible. [illegible] 5-30 pm and 7-30 pm trains at High Wood [illegible]. At 9 pm an impenetrable fog descended, and it was almost impossible to move, even on a road. Both parties [illegible] lost their way in the fog and did not arrive at Mametz Wood Camp until the small hours.	
	23/11/16		Section B & Headquarters in huts in Mametz Wood Camp. [illegible] Remainder cleaning kit.	

2449 Wt. W14957/M90 750,000 1/16 J.B.C. & A. Forms/C.2118/12.

Instructions regarding War Diaries and Intelligence Summaries are contained in F. S. Regs., Part II. and the Staff Manual respectively. Title Pages will be prepared in manuscript.

WAR DIARY
or ~~INTELLIGENCE SUMMARY~~

No 1 COMPANY MACHINE GUN CORPS

(Erase heading not required.)

Army Form C. 2118.

Place	Date	Hour	Summary of Events and Information	Remarks and references to Appendices
	22/11/16		2/Lieut Rhode joined from base depot	
			2/ " Mackenzie rejoined from hospital	
	24/11/16		~~Section~~ B on Fatigue 10 men. Remainder cleaning camp, overhauling guns & ammunition	
			2/Lieut Rhode took over A. Section from C.S.M. Soutar	
			Transport inspected, & incinerator built	
	23/11/16		Company on fatigue	
	25/11/16		C.Q.M.S Hart left for Blendecques	
			Major Angell. 2/Lieut Drake & 2/Lieut Baisen returned from Isolation Hospital	
	26/11/16		R.C. Service, Remainder of Company on fatigue	
			Lieut Snowball rejoined from leave	
	27/11/16		Company (less transport) moved to tents & dug-outs at Bazentin le Grand	
	28/11/16		" moved to huts at Bazentin-le-Petit.	
			2/Lieut A.G.D. McKay joined from base depot	
	29/11/16		Company on fatigue Camp shelled at mid-day	
			O.R. wounded	
	30/11/16		Company on fatigue	

[signature] Lieut

1st Brigade.

1st Division.

1st MACHINE GUN COMPANY ::: DECEMBER 1916.

Instructions regarding War Diaries and Intelligence Summaries are contained in F. S. Regs., Part II. and the Staff Manual respectively. Title Pages will be prepared in manuscript.

WAR DIARY

~~or~~

~~INTELLIGENCE SUMMARY~~

(Erase heading not required.)

Army Form C. 2118.

Vol 12

No 1 COMPANY MACHINE GUN CORPS

Place	Date	Hour	Summary of Events and Information	Remarks and references to Appendices
IN THE FIELD	1/12/16	JM	Company on fatigue No 4 Section, under Lieut. Bailey & 2/Lieut McKay with four guns relieved No 3 Company (composite) in the line. A German wiring party was caught by one of our guns under Sergt. Cullen & dispersed. Cries were heard, & the work was discontinued Position of Guns M.24.a.5.5. M.24.a.2.7. M.24.a.1.8. M.23.b.8.8. Section rejoined from Composite Company.	
"	2/12/16	JM	H.Q. in the line moved to dugout in Chalk deviation of PIONEER ALLEY M.23.d.4.6. Position of Guns M.24.a.5.5. M.23.b.8.8. M.23.d.4.6. M.29.b.3½.3½. Chalk trench heavily shelled during the night.	
"	3/12/16	JM	Positions slightly altered. No1. M.23.b.8.8. No2. M.23.b.4.5. No3. M.23.d.5.8. No4. M.29.b.0.8. Situation Normal.	
"	4/12/16	JM	Heavy bombardment of our lines between 4 & 5-30 A.M. No 1 Section under Lieut Atkinson & Lieut Lister relieved No4 SECTION in the afternoon. Two guns from No2 SECTION under Sergt. Lamond were taken up to occupy strong posts at F.H.G. These posts are not yet made, & the men have to dig emplacements & shelters temporarily. Position of Guns. No1. 2. 3. & 4. Unaltered F. M.30.a.0.5.0.5. G M.29.b.3½.2½.	
"	5/12/16	JM	Indirect fire carried out on tracks & dumps, in rear of enemy lines Work proceeding on emplacements & shelters. Position of Guns unaltered	

2449 Wt. W14957/M90 750,000 1/16 J.B.C. & A. Forms/C.2118/12.

Instructions regarding War Diaries and Intelligence Summaries are contained in F. S. Regs., Part II. and the Staff Manual respectively. Title Pages will be prepared in manuscript.

Army Form C. 2118.

WAR DIARY

~~or~~

~~INTELLIGENCE SUMMARY~~

(Erase heading not required.)

No1 COMPANY MACHINE GUN CORPS.

Place	Date	Hour	Summary of Events and Information	Remarks and references to Appendices
IN THE FIELD	6/12/16	JH	Indirect fire on tracks & dumps in rear of enemy lines Work as usual Position of Guns unaltered	
"	7/12/16	JH	Indirect fire & work as usual. No3 SECTION under Lieut Mackenzie & 2/Lieut Mohde relieved No1 SECTION, & 2 guns of No2 SECTION under Corporal Johnson relieved the other 2 guns of No2 SECTION Intermittent hostile shelling M.G fire reported near No1 & 3 guns. No2 Gun moved. Position of guns No1. M.24.a.0.4. No2. M.23.a.9.4. No3. M.23.d.5.8. No4. M.29.b.0.7. G. F.	
"	8/12/16	JH	Indirect fire as usual. Enemy M.G's replied Work proceeding as usual. Dug-out entrance at H.Q. blown in twice Position of Guns unaltered.	
"	9/12/16	JH	Indirect fire as usual, Work proceeding Hostile shelling & M.G. fire fairly heavy. No3 position damaged	
"	10/12/16	JH	Work proceeding as usual. No4 SECTION & part of No2 relieved guns in the line. Lieut Fiske & 2/Lieut McKay in charge Major J. Angell relinquished command of Company & proceeded to Grantham.	
	11/12/16	JH	Indirect fire & work as usual	
"	12/12/16	JH	Indirect fire & work as usual Position of guns No1 & No2 as before No3 M.23.d.5.9. No4 M.23.d.4.7. No5 M.29.b.0.7. G. one gun	

2449 Wt. W14957/M90 750,000 1/16 J.B.C.& A. Forms/C.2118/12.

Instructions regarding War Diaries and Intelligence Summaries are contained in F. S. Regs., Part II. and the Staff Manual respectively. Title Pages will be prepared in manuscript.

WAR DIARY

~~or~~

~~INTELLIGENCE SUMMARY~~

(Erase heading not required.)

Army Form C. 2118.

No 1 COMPANY. MACHINE GUN CORPS.

Place	Date	Hour	Summary of Events and Information	Remarks and references to Appendices
IN THE FIELD	13/12/16	JJS	Lieut. Atkinson & Lieut. Rohde with No 1 SECTION & part of No 2 relieved guns in the line. Two more guns sent up & manned by No 2 SECTION. Lieut. Atkinson took charge of front 4 guns & Lieut. Rohde of rear four.	
			Position of guns. No 1. M.24.a.0.4. No 2. M.23.a.9.5.4.5. No 3 M.23.d.4.9. No 4 M.23.d.4.7 No 5. M.22.a.9.5. G. F.	
			Shelling between No 2 position & EAUCOURT L'ABBAYE.	
"	14/12/16	JJS	Work proceeding as usual. No 3 position shelled. No 1 position subjected to M.G. & trench mortar fire.	
			Engineers worked on H.Q. dugout.	
			Situation quiet. Position of guns unchanged.	
"	15/12/16	JJS	A bombardment by Trench Mortars & artillery of the Maze & salient in M.24.a & c. took place at 2 A.M. At 2.1 A.M. 3 of our M.G's opened fire on the following targets	
			i. BLUECUT. (Rd running S.W. from post No 2. M.18.a.&c.)	
			ii. Sunken Rd in M.18.d.	
			iii. Area in M.18.d.0.5.	
			Firing was done from	
			2 hr. 1. to 2 hr. 3'	
			" 5' to " 7'	
			" 12' to " 14'	
			" 21' to " 23'	
			" 35' to " 37'	
			Owing to wind being unfavourable no gas was used	
			No 3 position shelled & position partially destroyed. Heavy shelling at No 5 & 6 positions	

2449 Wt. W14957/M90 750,000 1/16 J.B.C. & A. Forms/C.2118/12.

Army Form C. 2118.

Instructions regarding War Diaries and Intelligence Summaries are contained in F. S. Regs., Part II. and the Staff Manual respectively. Title Pages will be prepared in manuscript.

WAR DIARY
or
~~INTELLIGENCE SUMMARY~~

(Erase heading not required.)

Place	Date	Hour	Summary of Events and Information	Remarks and references to Appendices
IN THE FIELD	15/12/16	JH	Position of guns unaltered 1.O.R. admitted to hospital (sick) 1.O.R. returned from hospital	
	16/12/16	JH	Indirect fire & work as usual Considerable shelling at No3 & 4 positions. Lieut Mackenzie with No3 & 4 SECTIONS relieved Lieut Atkinson, & No1 & 2 SECTIONS in the line Position of guns as before 1.O.R. returned from hospital.	
"	17/12/16	JH	Indirect fire & work as usual. Fairly heavy shelling at night. Tear shells used near H.Q. dug-out. Lieut Lister relieved Lieut Rohde. Position of guns as before 1.O.R. evacuated (sick)	
"	18/12/16	JH	Indirect fire & work as usual PIONEER ALLEY nr. HEXHAM RD. heavily shelled. 2.O.R. admitted to hospital (sick) 1.O.R. evacuated (sick)	
	19/12/16	JH	Indirect fire & work as usual Situation fairly normal. Trench mortar fired at No1 POSITION The gun positions now definitely settled as follows. No1. M.24. a.0.4 No3 M.23. d.4.9. No5. M.29. a.9.5 F. (1 gun) M.30. a 05.05. No2. M.23. a.9½.4½. No4 M.23. d.4.7. G. (2 guns) M.29. b. 3½.2½.	

2449 Wt. W14957/M90 750,000 1/16 J.B.C. & A. Forms/C.2118/12.

Army Form C. 2118.

WAR DIARY

~~or~~

~~INTELLIGENCE SUMMARY~~

(Erase heading not required.)

Instructions regarding War Diaries and Intelligence Summaries are contained in F. S. Regs., Part II. and the Staff Manual respectively. Title Pages will be prepared in manuscript.

Place	Date	Hour	Summary of Events and Information	Remarks and references to Appendices
IN THE FIELD	19/12/16	JB	There was practically no emplacements or shelters when the Company took over the line on 1/12/16 & the following have been, or are being made up to date	
			No 1 2 emplacements	
			No 2 2 emplacements 1 shelter	
			No 3 2 emplacements	
			No 4 2 emplacements 1 also for anti, aircraft	
			No 5 3. emplacements	
			G 4. emplacements & anti aircraft	
			F 3. emplacements 1 dugout	
			2. O.R. admitted to hospital (sick) 5. O.R. joined from the base	
			3. O.R. evacuated (sick)	
"	20/12/16	JB	Lieut. T. A. Hill from 151st M.G.C. assumed command of the Company.	
			Indirect fire & work as usual	
			Between 10 & 11 A.M. some German aeroplanes came over our lines. They were heavily fired on by our guns, at No 4 & G. they retired very rapidly over their own lines	
			Lieut Atkinson & Rohde with No 1 SECTION (rear 4 guns) (No 2 SECTION forward 4 guns relieved No 3 & No 4. SECTIONS in the line.	
			Fairly heavy shelling. F. shelled by gas shells.	
			2. O.R. evacuated (sick)	
			1. O.R. returned from hospital	
"	21/12/16	JB	At 3.30 A.M. Trench mortar & artillery bombarded the MAZE with lethal, lachrymatory & ordinary shells. 3 of our guns fired as follows	
			i BLUECUT (Road running S.W. from POST No 2. M.18.a.6.7.c.)	
			ii SUNKEN ROAD in M.18.D.	
			iii TRACKS 9 IN M.18.a.	

Instructions regarding War Diaries and Intelligence Summaries are contained in F. S. Regs., Part II. and the Staff Manual respectively. Title Pages will be prepared in manuscript.

WAR DIARY
or
~~INTELLIGENCE SUMMARY~~

(Erase heading not required.)

Army Form C. 2118.

Place	Date	Hour	Summary of Events and Information	Remarks and references to Appendices
IN THE FIELD	21/12/16	JSS	Fire was carried out at following times 3.30. to 3.31. 33. to 35. 40. to 42. 47 to 48. 4.10 to 4.13. Before & afterwards indirect fire as usual Intermittent enemy shelling.	
	22/12/16	JSS	Indirect fire & work as usual. Enemy artillery very active No.2 gun feed block damaged. No.4. Barrel casing pierced 1.O.R. admitted to hospital (sick)	
	23/12/16	JSS	Indirect fire & work as usual Enemy shelling fairly heavy. L/C. Athya & 2 men buried in a dug-out at G. but got out. Emplacement (at No5 destroyed. 2.O.R. admitted to hospital (sick)	
	24/12/16	JSS	Indirect fire & work as usual Fairly heavy shelling at night especially near G gun, about 8 & 9.P.M. Dugout at No4 [illegible] up to H.Q. Lieut Mackenzie with No3 SECTION & Lieut [illegible] with No4 SECTION relieved No1 & 2 SECTIONS in the line. Lieut Bailey & 5.O.R. proceed to M.G SCHOOL, CAMIERS. ON COURSE 1. O.R. admitted to hospital (sick) 1. O.R. evacuated (sick) 1. O.R. returned from hospital.	

2449 Wt. W14957/M90 750,000 1/16 J.B.C. & A. Forms/C.2118/12.

Army Form C. 2118.

*Instructions regarding War Diaries and Intelligence Summaries are contained in F. S. Regs., Part II. and the Staff Manual respectively. Title Pages will be prepared in manuscript.

WAR DIARY

~~or~~

~~INTELLIGENCE SUMMARY~~

(Erase heading not required.)

Place	Date	Hour	Summary of Events and Information	Remarks and references to Appendices
IN THE FIELD	25/12/16	JHS	No indirect fire between 12 P.M. & 12 P.M. Enemy shelling somewhat less all day.	
"	26/12/16	JHS	Indirect fire & work as usual Several enemy aeroplanes were fired on during the morning & driven to their own lines 1 O.R. admitted to hospital (sick)	
"	27/12/16	JHS	Indirect fire & work as usual. Intermittent but not heavy shelling.	
"	28/12/16	JHS	Indirect fire & work as usual. Situation normal Fairly heavy shelling at night Lieut Atkinson & Rohde with No1 & 2 SECTIONS relieved NO 3 & 4 SECTIONS in the line NO1 SECTION in the 4 forward positions	
"	29/12/16	JHS	Company relieved by NO 149 MACHINE GUN COMPANY. Headquarters moved to Tent Camp at N.E. CORNER OF MAMETZ WOOD Guns relieved in the afternoon No casualties (except slightly wounded & remained at Duty) suffered during the month's tour in the line 1 O.R. admitted to hospital (sick) 16 O.R. joined from the base	
"	30/12/16	JHS	Company cleaning guns & packing limbers &c.	
"	31/12/16	JHS	Company moved via MAMETZ, FRICOURT to ALBERT. Headquarters & officers at No 51. Rue de Bapaume, Sections at Rue des Grandes Marais. Transport west of Albert just off AMIENS ROAD	

J.S. Snowball.
LIEUT & ADJT.
NO1 MACHINE GUN COMPANY

2449 Wt. W14957/M90 750,000 1/16 J.B.C. & A. Forms/C.2118/12.

1ST DIVISION
1ST INFY BDE

NO. 1 MACHINE GUN COY.

JAN - DEC 1917

W A R   D I A R Y.

No.1. Machine Gun Coy.

1st. INFANTRY BRIGADE.

1st. DIVISION.

JANUARY. 1917.

Army Form C. 2118.

Instructions regarding War Diaries and Intelligence Summaries are contained in F. S. Regs., Part II. and the Staff Manual respectively. Title Pages will be prepared in manuscript.

WAR DIARY
or
~~INTELLIGENCE SUMMARY~~

No1 MACHINE (Erase heading not required.) GUN COMPANY.

Vol 13

Place	Date	Hour	Summary of Events and Information	Remarks and references to Appendices
In the field	1/1/17	JH	Company Training, Cleaning Guns, Kit &c	
			London Gazette:-	
			Military Cross. 2nd Lieut (Temp. Major) J. Argell. S. Lancs Regt. attached M. G. Corps.	
			" " 2nd Lieut (Temp Lieut) J. C. Murley, London Regt. attached M. G. Corps.	
			Mentioned. 2nd Lieut (Temp Lieut) J. W. Garden Royal Highlanders attached M. G. Corps.	
			" Coy. Q.M.S. P. McHart. Machine Gun Corps	
			1. O.R. admitted to hospital	
"	2/1/17.	JH	Company Training. Company inspected by Commanding Officer. 2. O.R. evacuated.	
"	3/1/17.	JH	Company cleaning limbers &c, N.C.O's under instruction.	
"	4/1/17.	JH	" " " " 2. O.R. admitted to hospital.	
"	5/1/17	JH	Company Training.	
			2. O.R. admitted to hospital.	
			1. O.R. returned from hospital.	
"	6/1/17	JH	Company Training.	
"	7/1/17	JH	Church Parade	
			3. O.R. admitted to hospital.	
"	8/1/17	JH	Company Training	
			1. O.R. admitted to hospital.	
"	9/1/17	JH	Company Training	
			1. O.R. returned from hospital.	
	10/1/17	JH	Company Training. 1. O.R. returned from hospital.	

2449 Wt. W14957/M90 750,000 1/16 J.B.C. & A. Forms/C.2118/12.

Army Form C. 2118.

WAR DIARY
or
~~INTELLIGENCE SUMMARY~~

(Erase heading not required.)

Instructions regarding War Diaries and Intelligence Summaries are contained in F. S. Regs., Part II. and the Staff Manual respectively. Title Pages will be prepared in manuscript.

No. 1 MACHINE GUN COMPANY.

Place	Date	Hour	Summary of Events and Information	Remarks and references to Appendices
In the field	11/1/17	JSS	Company Training.	
"	12/1/17	JSS	Company Training, and bathing. 2/Lieut. J.S. Taylor joined from the base. 1. O.R. returned from hospital.	
"	13/1/17	JSS	Company Training.	
"	14/1/17	JSS	Church parades. 2. O.R. admitted to hospital.	
"	15/1/17	JSS	Company Training. 4. O.R. evacuated (sick)	
"	16/1/17	JSS	Company Training 1. O.R. evacuated (sick)	
"	17/1/17	JSS	Company Training, Company inspected by Commanding Officer 1. O.R. admitted to hospital 1. O.R. returned from "	
"	18/1/17	JSS	Company Training 1. O.R. joined Company from the base. 1. O.R. evacuated. (sick)	
"	19/1/17	JSS	Company Training 1. O.R. evacuated (sick)	
"	20/1/17	JSS	Company Training 2 O.R. evacuated sick)	

2449 Wt. W14957/M90 750,000 1/16 J.B.C. & A. Forms/C.2118/12.

Army Form C. 2118.

Instructions regarding War Diaries and Intelligence Summaries are contained in F. S. Regs., Part II. and the Staff Manual respectively. Title Pages will be prepared in manuscript.

WAR DIARY
or
~~INTELLIGENCE SUMMARY~~

(Erase heading not required.)

No. 1. MACHINE GUN COMPANY

Place	Date	Hour	Summary of Events and Information	Remarks and references to Appendices
In the field	21/1/17	JS	Church parades	
			1. O.R. admitted to hospital	
			1. O.R. returned from "	
"	22/1/17	JS	Company Training - packing limbers &c	
			3. O.R. admitted to hospital	
"	23/1/17	JS	Company moved into billets at Warloy	
			(ROUTE. LAVIEVILLE - HENENCOURT	
	24/1/17	JS	Company Training.	
"	25/1/17	JS	Company Training	
			1. O.R. admitted to hospital	
"	26/1/17	JS	Company Training	
			1 O.R. joined from Base	
			1 O.R. evacuated sick	
			1 O.R. admitted to hospital	
	27/1/17	JS	Company Training	
			1. O.R. admitted to hospital	
	28/1/17	JS	No parades (Sunday)	
	29/1/17	JS	Company training	
			1. O.R. admitted to hospital	
	30/1/17	JS	Company training	
	31/1/17	JS	Company training	

J. S. [illegible]
Lieut & Adjt
No 1 Machine Gun Coy

2449 Wt. W14957/M90 750,000 1/16 J.B.C. & A. Forms/C.2118/12.

W A R   D I A R Y.

No.1. MACHINE GUN COMPANY.

1st. INFANTRY BRIGADE.

1st. DIVISION.

FEBRUARY. 1917.

Army Form C. 2118.

*Instructions regarding War Diaries and Intelligence Summaries are contained in F. S. Regs., Part II. and the Staff Manual respectively. Title Pages will be prepared in manuscript.

WAR DIARY
or
~~INTELLIGENCE SUMMARY~~

No1 MACHINE *(Erase heading not required.)* GUN COMPANY.

Vol 14

Place	Date	Hour	Summary of Events and Information	Remarks and references to Appendices
In the field	1/2/17	JHS	Company Training	
			1. O.R. evacuated (sick)	
"	2/2/17	JHS	Company Training	
			2 O.R. admitted to hospital	
"	3/2/17	JHS	Brigade tactical scheme	
			1. O.R. evacuated sick.	
"	4/2/17	JHS	Company moved via BASIEUX, MERICOURT, DERNACOURT, SAILLY-LE-SEC, SAILLY LAURETTE to billets in HAMEL (HUTS)	
"	5/2/17	JHS	Company Training	
			1. O.R. admitted to hospital	
			1 O.R. returned from "	
			1. O.R. evacuated sick	
"	6/2/17	JHS	Company training	
			1. O.R. admitted to (hospital)	
"	7/2/17	JHS	Company moved via CERISY, MERICOURT TO CAMP 52 (NEAR CHUIGNOLLES, ON PROYART ROAD)	
			Brigade inspected on the march by G.O.C. 24TH FRENCH DIVISION & G.O.C. 1ST DIVISION.	
"	8/2/17	JHS	Company Training	
"	9/2/17	JHS	Company Training	
"	10/2/17	JHS	Company Training	
			1. O.R. admitted to hospital.	

2449 Wt. W14957/M90 750,000 1/16 J.B.C. & A. Forms/C.2118/12.

Army Form C. 2118.

WAR DIARY
or
~~INTELLIGENCE SUMMARY~~

Instructions regarding War Diaries and Intelligence Summaries are contained in F. S. Regs., Part II. and the Staff Manual respectively. Title Pages will be prepared in manuscript.

No1. MACHINE (*Erase heading not required.*) GUN COMPANY

Place	Date	Hour	Summary of Events and Information	Remarks and references to Appendices
In the field	11/2/17	JH	Route March.	
"	12/2/17	JH	Company moved via CHUIGNOLLES TO CHUIGNES IN HUTS.	
"	13/2/17	JH	Transport moved to CUISINE WOOD.	
			Company relieved No2. M.G. COY. in the line, proceeding via DOMPIERRE and ASSEVILLERS.	
			Three sections in front & support lines, one in Reserve line.	
			No1 SECTION under Lieut. G. P. W. Atkinson in centre.	
			No2 " " 2/Lieut. G. G. A. McKay on left.	
			No3 " " " J. S. Taylor in reserve line.	
			No4 " " Lieut R. L. Bailey on right.	
			GUN POSITIONS (Ref MAPS. DOMPIERRE and BARLEUX 1/10,000)	
			No4 SECTION	
			RIGHT GUNS. 1. N.28.d.6.9.	
			2. N.28.d.6½.9½.	
			3. N.28.d. 2.8.	
			4. N.28.b. 2.0.	
			CENTRE GUNS 1. N.28.b.2.5.	
			2. N.28.b.2.6.	
			3. N.22.d.5.0½.	
			4. N.22.d.6½.4½.	
			HQ for RIGHT & CENTRE N.28.b.2.5.	

2449 Wt. W14957/M90 750,000 1/16 J.B.C. & A. Forms/C.2118/12.

Army Form C. 2118.

Instructions regarding War Diaries and Intelligence Summaries are contained in F. S. Regs., Part II. and the Staff Manual respectively. Title Pages will be prepared in manuscript.

WAR DIARY
or
~~INTELLIGENCE SUMMARY~~

No 1 MACHINE (Erase heading not required.) GUN COMPANY

Place	Date	Hour	Summary of Events and Information	Remarks and references to Appendices
In the field	13/2/17	JH	LEFT GUNS 1. N.22. b. 7½.2½.	
			2. N.16. c. 8.2. (In reserve used as A.-A.)	
			3. N.23. a. 07.	
			4. N.22. b. 9.8.	
			LEFT. H.Q. N.22. b. 5.9	
			RESERVE LINE. 1. N 22. a. 6.2. (used as Anti-Aircraft)	
			2. N 22. a. 5.9.	
			3. N 16. d. 2.5.	
			4. N 16. b. 1½.5.	
			COMPANY H.Q. N 15 d. 4.5.	
			Relief completed at 7 A.M. on 14th.	
"	14/2/17	JH	Trenches reconnoitred, positions checked &c.	
"	15/2/17	JH	Hostile planes fired on at intervals by our anti-aircraft guns	
"	16/2/17	JH	Hostile planes fired on. A little hostile shelling. No 2 Left position hit.	
"	17/2/17	JH	Thick mist little enemy artillery activity	
			1 O.R. evacuated (sick)	
"	18/2/17	JH	Relief. No 1 Section (Lieut Atkinson) took over 4 guns on right	
			No 3 Section (Lieut Taylor) took over 4 guns on left	
			No 2 Section (Lieut McKay) took over 4 guns in reserve line	
			No 4 Section (Lieut Bailey) in reserve at Company H.Q.	

2449 Wt. W14957/M90 750,000 1/16 J.B.C. & A. Forms/C.2118/12.

Army Form C. 2118

WAR DIARY
or
~~INTELLIGENCE SUMMARY~~

(Erase heading not required.) No1 MACHINE GUN COMPANY.

Instructions regarding War Diaries and Intelligence Summaries are contained in F. S. Regs., Part II. and the Staff Manual respectively. Title Pages will be prepared in manuscript.

Place	Date	Hour	Summary of Events and Information	Remarks and references to Appendices
In the field	18/2/17	JH	GUN POSITIONS No1 N.28. d. 6.9½. } " 2. N.28. b. 2.6. } No1. SECTION " 3. N.22. d. 5.0½. } " 4. N.28. d. 5.9. } " 5. N.22 d 6.5. } " 6. N.22. b 75.10. } No3. SECTION " 7. N.22. b. 10.8. } " 8. N.22. b. 95.90. } R.1 } R.2 } Positions unchanged. No2 SECTION. R.3 } R.4 }	
"	19/2/17	JH	GUN POSITIONS No1 N.28. d. 5.8. 2 N.28 b. 5.2 3 N.28. a. 9.6. 4 N.22. d. 45.5. 5 } 6 } unchanged. 7 } 8 } 1 O.R. evacuated wounded	
"	20/2/17	JH	Situation quiet 1. O.R. evacuated wounded.	

2449 Wt. W14957/M90 750,000 1/16 J.B.C. & A. Forms/C.2118/12.

Army Form C. 2118.

Instructions regarding War Diaries and Intelligence Summaries are contained in F. S. Regs., Part II. and the Staff Manual respectively. Title Pages will be prepared in manuscript.

WAR DIARY
or
~~INTELLIGENCE SUMMARY~~

(Erase heading not required.)

No1 MACHINE GUN COMPANY

Place	Date	Hour	Summary of Events and Information	Remarks and references to Appendices
In the field	21/2/17	JHS	No4 Section (Lieut R. L. Bailey) relieved No1 SECTION in the line	
			No1 Section came into reserve.	
"	22/2/17	JHS	Emplacement at R.2 finished. Alternative emplacement for R.4. made	
"	23/2/17	JHS	S.O.S. went up by Brigade on right about 8 p.m. Some shelling on our own front.	
			1. O.R. evacuated (wounded)	
"	24/2/17	JHS	Situation quiet	
			Relief.	
			No1 SECTION on right	
			No2 " " left	
			No4 " reserve line	
			No3 " in reserve.	
"	25/2/17	JHS	Hostile aeroplane fired upon.	
			1000 rounds fired by No R.2. gun on road in N.24.c.	
			1 O.R. evacuated (wounded)	
"	26/2/17	JHS	Lieut. Mackenzie relieved Lieut. Bailey	
	27/2/17	JHS	Situation quiet.	
"	28/2/17	JHS.	No4 SECTION with one gun and No3 SECTION with two guns co-operated in a smoke attack by firing on 1. Road in H.24.c. 2. FOURNAISE ALLEY. H.29. b. & d.	

2449 Wt. W14957/M90 750,000 1/16 J.B.C. & A. Forms/C.2118/12.

Army Form C. 2118.

Instructions regarding War Diaries and Intelligence Summaries are contained in F. S. Regs., Part II. and the Staff Manual respectively. Title Pages will be prepared in manuscript.

WAR DIARY
or
~~INTELLIGENCE SUMMARY~~
(Erase heading not required.)

No1. MACHINE GUN COMPANY

Place	Date	Hour	Summary of Events and Information	Remarks and references to Appendices
In the field	28/2/17	[illegible]	3. Trench junction at N.30.C.1.7. Firing continued from 5.25 to 5.55 AM. Our artillery also co-operated. Enemy retaliated with artillery and M.G's	

J. A. Snowball
LIEUT. & ADJT.
No1 MACHINE GUN COMPANY.

2449 Wt. W14957/M90 750,000 1/16 J.B.C. & A. Forms/C.2118/12.

W A R   D I A R Y.

No.1. MACHINE GUN COMPANY.

1st. INFANTRY BRIGADE.

1st. DIVISION.

MARCH, 1917.

Army Form C. 2118.

Instructions regarding War Diaries and Intelligence Summaries are contained in F. S. Regs., Part II. and the Staff Manual respectively. Title Pages will be prepared in manuscript.

WAR DIARY
or
~~INTELLIGENCE SUMMARY~~
(Erase heading not required.)

No 1. Machine Gun Company.

Vol 15

Place	Date	Hour	Summary of Events and Information	Remarks and references to Appendices
In the Field	1.3.17	JHS	Company relieved by No 3. Machine Gun Coy. Relief completed at about 2 am. on 2nd. Company went into billets at CHUIGNES.	
			1. OR. admitted to hospital (sick)	
			5 O.R. joined from Base depot.	
	2.3.17	JHS	Company bathed.	
	3.3.17	JHS	Company cleaning clothing, gun kit. etc.	
	4.3.17	JHS	Route march.	
	5.3.17	JHS	Inspection by C.O.	
	6.3.17.	JHS	Company training.	
	7.3.17	JHS	Company training. Box respirators fitted.	
	8.3.17	JHS	Inspection by Brigade of Company with Transport.	
	9.3.17	JHS	Company training	
	10.3.17	JHS	Morning, packing limbers. No 2 Section, under Lieut. Rohde relieved A. Section No 2 Machine Gun Coy. at Telegraph Camp at 4pm. Remaining sections moved up to the line between 10 pm. & 12 midnight.	
			7 O.R. joined from Base depot.	

2449 Wt. W14957/M90 750,000 1/16 J.B.C. & A. Forms/C.2118/12.

Instructions regarding War Diaries and Intelligence Summaries are contained in F. S. Regs., Part II. and the Staff Manual respectively. Title Pages will be prepared in manuscript.

WAR DIARY
or
~~INTELLIGENCE SUMMARY~~
(Erase heading not required.)

No1. Machine Gun Company.

Army Form C. 2118.

Place	Date	Hour	Summary of Events and Information	Remarks and references to Appendices
In the Field.	11.3.17	JH	Relief of No2. Machine Gun Company completed at 4 am. Six ~~guns~~ guns were in the front + support lines & six guns were in the Reserve line.	
			No 3. Section (3 guns) under Lieut. Mackenzie on right front.	
			No 4 Section (3 guns) under Lieut. Lister on left front.	
			No 1 Section (4 guns) and remaining guns of Nos. 3+4 Sections under 2/Lt. McKay in Reserve line.	
			H.Q. off MEUDON ALLEY behind Support Trenches.	
	12.3.17	JH	Making up trench stores, reconnoitering trenches etc. Situation normal.	
	13.3.17	JH	Indirect fire carried out on Cross Roads in O13a. Several fires were observed behind the enemy lines. Some enemy shelling during the night particularly about 1.30 AM. to 3 AM. A few gas shells were fired.	
			2/Lieut Melville. P.S. joined Company from base depot.	
	14.3.17	JH	No 2 Section relieved No 3. Section with 3. guns in the front System under Lieut McKay, and one gun in the Reserve line. No 3. Section returned to Telegraph Camp under Lieut. Rohde. No 1 section relieved the 3 guns of No 4 Section in the front system with 3 guns under 2/Lieut Taylor. Lieut. Lister had command of guns in Reserve line which now consisted of No 4 Section, 4 guns, Nos. 1 + 2 Sections, 1 gun each. ~~Ref~~ Relief was commenced at 7 PM. and completed about 4 AM. Usual fired behind enemy lines.	

2449 Wt. W14957/M90 750,000 1/16 J.B.C. & A. Forms/C.2118/12.

Army Form C. 2118.

WAR DIARY
or
~~INTELLIGENCE SUMMARY~~ No. 1. Machine Gun. Company.

(Erase heading not required.)

Instructions regarding War Diaries and Intelligence Summaries are contained in F. S. Regs., Part II. and the Staff Manual respectively. Title Pages will be prepared in manuscript.

Place	Date	Hour	Summary of Events and Information	Remarks and references to Appendices
In the Field.	15.3.17	JSS	Indirect fire carried out on Cross Roads in O13a. Intermittent shelling of gun position about 11 b. 4.4½. Usual fires were seen.	
	16.3.17.	JSS	No 3 Section under 2/Lt. P.S. Melville vacated Telegraph Camp and were billeted in dugouts in bank at N4d. No 3. Gun was moved to N17a33 to fire to left to cover gap which was to be left in our line from near hedge to N17b49. No 4 gun was moved close to No 5 gun in ROUMANIA support line to cover this gap from the right. Enemy shelling Reserve line & area in front about 6.0 P.M. at very long range. Gas shells were used. Indirect fire was carried out during the night on, i. Cross Roads in O.13a 6.5. ii. Dump O.13d 1.1. Company H.Q. moved to FLAUCOURT. 1. O.R. Killed in Action. 1. O.R. wounded.	
	17.3.17.	JSS	In order to assist operations of troops on our right indirect fire was carried out at 7 AM. on. i. Cross Roads in O13a 6.5. ii. Dump in O13d 1.1. Three guns were used and 1500 rounds were fired.	

2449 Wt. W14957/M90 750,000 1/16 J.B.C. & A. Forms/C.2118/12.

Army Form C. 2118.

Instructions regarding War Diaries and Intelligence Summaries are contained in F. S. Regs., Part II. and the Staff Manual respectively. Title Pages will be prepared in manuscript.

WAR DIARY
or
~~INTELLIGENCE SUMMARY~~
(Erase heading not required.)

No. 1. Machine Gun Company.

Place	Date	Hour	Summary of Events and Information	Remarks and references to Appendices
In the Field	17.3.17.	JH	About 7 am. the 1st Camerons entered the enemy trenches & shortly afterwards the Gloucesters also did. Before noon our patrols had reached the River Somme. Lieut. Lister with 4 guns (No 4 Section) was placed at disposal of left Batt'n (1st Camerons) Lieut. Melville & No 3 Section were placed at disposal of O.C. 10th Gloucesters.	
			1. O.R. Admitted to Hospital (sick)	
			1. O.R. Evacuated. (sick)	
			1. O.R. Joined from base depot.	
	18.3.17	JH	Two guns of No 3 Section & 2 guns of No 4 section were pushed forward to EGLANTINE Trench to cover the Somme. Remaining two guns of No 3. Section were placed on high ground S of BARLEUX, the remaining two of No 4 Section were placed north of BARLEUX. No 1 & 2 Section came into reserve at FLAUCOURT. Company H.Q. moved to MEUDON ALLEY (N3 d.9.2)	
			1 O.R. Admitted to Hospital (sick)	
	19.3.17	JH	The R. Berks crossed the Somme about 9 am. Our four guns in EGLANTINE Trench were ~~[illegible]~~ prepared to give covering fire.	
			Two rear guns of 3 & 4 Sections withdrawn into reserve at FLAUCOURT.	
			Two guns of Nos 1 & 2 Sections under Lieut. Mackenzie crossed the Somme about 4.30 PM. & were attached to the R Berks taking up positions in trench about 300 yds. west of the River. Remainder of Company on fatigue.	

Army Form C. 2118.

Instructions regarding War Diaries and Intelligence Summaries are contained in F. S. Regs., Part II. and the Staff Manual respectively. Title Pages will be prepared in manuscript.

WAR DIARY
or
~~INTELLIGENCE SUMMARY~~
(Erase heading not required.)

No 1. Machine Gun Company.

Place	Date	Hour	Summary of Events and Information	Remarks and references to Appendices
In the Field.	19.3.17	JH	1. O. R. admitted to Hospital (sick)	
			2/Lieut. McKay admitted to Hospital (sick)	
	20.3.17	JH	The four guns East of the River were moved forward about 500 yds. onto the high ground	
			1. O. R. admitted to Hospital (sick)	
	21.3.17	JH	Company moved into dug outs S.W. of HERBECOURT. H.Q. in old Brigade H.Q.	
	22.3.17	JH	Cleaning guns, kit etc.	
	23.3.17	JH	Company on fatigue at FAY.	
	24.3.17	JH	Company on fatigue at FAY.	
			2. O. R. rejoined from Hospital	
			1. O. R. evacuated. (sick)	
	25.3.17	JH	Company on fatigue at FAY.	
			1. O. R. admitted to Hospital (sick)	
			1. O. R. joined from 87th Company.	
	26.3.17	JH	Company on fatigue a FAY.	
			1. O. R. admitted to Hospital (sick)	

2449 Wt. W14957/M90 750,000 1/16 J.B.C. & A. Forms/C.2118/12.

Army Form C. 2118.

Instructions regarding War Diaries and Intelligence Summaries are contained in F. S. Regs., Part II. and the Staff Manual respectively. Title Pages will be prepared in manuscript.

WAR DIARY
or
INTELLIGENCE SUMMARY
(Erase heading not required.)

Place	Date	Hour	Summary of Events and Information	Remarks and references to Appendices
In the Field	27.3.17	JH	Company bathed at CHUIGNES.	
			1. O.R. Admitted to Hospital (Sick)	
	28.3.17	JH	Company inspected by Commanding Officer.	
			Cleaning & packing limbers.	
	29.3.17	JH	Company (less No 3 Section) moved via CUISINE WOOD, FOUCAUCOURT, FRAMERVILLE & VAUVILLERS to ROSIERES (in billets)	
			Two guns of No 3. Section under Lieut. Mackenzie relieved 2 guns of 50th Division at anti-aircraft post at FROISSY.	
			Two guns of No 3. Section under 2/Lt. Taylor relieved 2 guns of 50th Division at le PETIT BLAGNY (near AMIENS)	
	30.3.17	JH	Company cleaning billets equipment etc. and training.	
			2. O.R. admitted to Hospital. Lieut G H Lister admitted to Hospital.	
	31.3.17	JH	Company training	
			1. O.R. admitted to Hospital.	

J. S. Snowball
Lieut & Adjt
No 1 Machine Gun Coy

2449 Wt. W14957/M90 750,000 1/16 J.B.C. & A. Forms/C.2118/12.

W A R   D I A R Y.

No.1.MACHINE GUN COY.

1st.INFANTRY BRIGADE.

1st.DIVISION.

APRIL.1917.

Army Form C. 2118

Instructions regarding War Diaries and Intelligence Summaries are contained in F. S. Regs., Part II. and the Staff Manual respectively. Title Pages will be prepared in manuscript.

WAR DIARY
or
~~INTELLIGENCE SUMMARY~~

No1 MACHINE (Erase heading not required.) GUN COMPANY.

Vol 16

Place	Date	Hour	Summary of Events and Information	Remarks and references to Appendices
IN THE FIELD	1/4/17	JH	Company on fatigue:- Salvage work at Mancourt.	
			3. O.R. joined from base depot.	
			3. O.R. admitted into hospital (sick)	
"	2/4/17	JH	Company on fatigue:- Salving telephone wire round Mancourt, Meharicourt, VRELY & ROSIERES.	
			3. O.R. evacuated (sick)	
"	3/4/17	JH	Company on fatigue.	
"	4/4/17	JH	Company on fatigue	
"	5/4/17	JH	Company on fatigue.	
			1 O.R. evacuated (sick)	
"	6/4/17	JH	Company on fatigue.	
			1 O.R. admitted into hospital (sick)	
			1. O.R. evacuated (sick)	
"	7/4/17	JH	Company on fatigue	
			2. O.R. joined from base depot	
			1 O.R. admitted into hospital.	
"	8/4/17	JH	Company on fatigue.	
"	9/4/17	JH	Company on fatigue.	
			1 O.R. evacuated (sick)	
			1. O.R. rejoined from hospital.	
"	10/4/17	JH	Company on fatigue	

2449 Wt. W14957/M90 750,000 1/16 J.B.C. & A. Forms/C.2118/12.

Army Form C. 2118.

Instructions regarding War Diaries and Intelligence Summaries are contained in F. S. Regs., Part II. and the Staff Manual respectively. Title Pages will be prepared in manuscript.

WAR DIARY
or
~~INTELLIGENCE SUMMARY~~

No 7 MACHINE (*Erase heading not required.*) GUN COMPANY

Place	Date	Hour	Summary of Events and Information	Remarks and references to Appendices
IN THE FIELD	11/4/17	JH	Company on fatigue	
"	12/4/17	JH	Company on fatigue	
			2 O.R. admitted into hospital (sick)	
"	13/4/17	JH	Company on fatigue	
			1 O.R. rejoined from hospital	
"	14/4/17	JH	Company on fatigue	
			Transport inspected by Brigadier	
			2 O.R. admitted into hospital (sick)	
"	15/4/17	JH	Company on fatigue	
			1 O.R. joined from base depot.	
"	16/4/17	JH	Company moved via VAUVILLERS, FRAMERVILLE, PROYART, TO CHUIGNES. Company in huts	
			1 O.R. rejoined from hospital	
"	17/4/17	JH	Company cleaning kit &c	
			1 O.R. rejoined from hospital	
"	18/4/17	JH	Company training	
"	19/4/17	JH	Company training	
			2 O.R. joined from base depot	
			1 O.R. admitted to hospital (sick)	
"	20/4/17	JH	Company training	
			1 O.R. admitted to hospital (sick)	

2449 Wt. W14957/M90 750,000 1/16 J.B.C. & A. Forms/C.2118/12.

Army Form C. 2118.

Instructions regarding War Diaries and Intelligence Summaries are contained in F. S. Regs., Part II. and the Staff Manual respectively. Title Pages will be prepared in manuscript.

WAR DIARY

or

~~INTELLIGENCE SUMMARY~~

No 1 MACHINE *(Erase heading not required.)* GUN COMPANY

Place	Date	Hour	Summary of Events and Information	Remarks and references to Appendices
IN THE FIELD	21/4/17		Company Training 1. O.R. admitted to hospital (sick.)	
"	22/4/17		Church parades	
"	23/4/17		Company training	
"	24/4/17		Company training 1. O.R. rejoined from hospital	
"	25/4/17		Company training 1. O.R. evacuated (sick)	
"	26/4/17		Company training 1. O.R. rejoined from hospital	
"	27/4/17		Company training No 1 & 2 SECTIONS attached to 1st CAMERONS HIGHLANDERS for co-operation in attack scheme. 1. O.R. admitted to hospital (sick)	
"	28/4/17		Company training. No 4 SECTION attached to 10th GLOSTER REGT. for co-operation in attack scheme. 1. O.R. admitted to hospital (sick) 6. O.R. joined from base depot.	
"	29/4/17		Church parades	
"	30/4/17		Company training 1. O.R. admitted to hospital (sick)	

[illegible]
Lieut & Adjt
No 1 Machine Gun Coy

2449 Wt. W14957/M90 750,000 1/16 J.B.C. & A. Forms/C.2118/12.

W A R D I A R Y.

No.1.MACHINE GUN COMPANY.

1st.INFANTRY BRIGADE.

1st.DIVISION.

MAY.1917.

Army Form C. 2118.

Instructions regarding War Diaries and Intelligence Summaries are contained in F. S. Regs., Part II. and the Staff Manual respectively. Title Pages will be prepared in manuscript.

WAR DIARY
or
~~INTELLIGENCE SUMMARY~~

No1 MACHINE (*Erase heading not required.*) GUN COMPANY.

Vol 17

Place	Date	Hour	Summary of Events and Information	Remarks and references to Appendices
In the field	1/5/17		Company Training No1 & 3 SECTIONS attached to 1st Royal Highlanders (Black Watch) for scheme)	
"	2/5/17		Company Training No2 SECTIONS attached to 8th Royal Berks. Regt. for co-operation in scheme	
"	3/5/17		Company Training.	
"	4/5/17		Company Training No4 SECTION attached to 1st Royal Highlanders (Black Watch) and two guns No3 SECTION attached to 8th Royal Berks Regt. for tactical schemes	
"	5/5/17		Company Parades. (No3 SECTION attached to 1st Royal Highlanders (Black Watch) for co-operation in schemes.	
"	6/5/17		Church Parades.	
"	7/5/17		Company Training.	
"	8/5/17		Company Training No4 SECTION attached to 1st Royal Highlanders (Black Watch) for co-operation in tactical scheme.	
"	9/5/17		Company Training No4 SECTION attached to 10th Glosters Regt. for co-operation in tactical scheme.	
"	10/5/17		Company Training No1 SECTION attached to 1st Royal Highlanders (Black Watch) for co-operation in tactical scheme.	
"	11/5/17		Company Training No2 & 4 SECTIONS attached 1st Cameron's and 8th Royal Berks Regt. for co-operation in tactical scheme.	
"	12/5/17		Company Training Captain T.N. Hill handed over command of Company to Captain [illegible]	

2449 Wt. W14957/M90 750,000 1/16 J.B.C. & A. Forms/C.2118/12.

Army Form C. 2118.

Instructions regarding War Diaries and Intelligence Summaries are contained in F. S. Regs., Part II. and the Staff Manual respectively. Title Pages will be prepared in manuscript.

WAR DIARY
or
~~INTELLIGENCE SUMMARY~~

No1. MACHINE *(Erase heading not required.)* GUN COMPANY

Place	Date	Hour	Summary of Events and Information	Remarks and references to Appendices
In the field	13/5/17		Church Parades	MF
"	14/5/17		Company Training	MF
			LIEUT. G. H. LISTER admitted into hospital (sick)	MF
"	15/5/17		Company Training	
"	16/5/17		Company paraded for co-operation in Brigade tactical scheme	MF
			1. O.R. evacuated (sick)	MF
"	17/5/17		Company Training	MF
"	18/5/17		Company Training	
			1 O.R. admitted into hospital (sick)	MF
"	19/5/17		Company moved to BAYONVILLERS	
"	20/5/17		Company Training	MF
			1. O.R. evacuated (sick)	MF
"	21/5/17		Company Training	MF
"	22/5/17		Company Training	
"	23/5/17		Company Training	
			1. O.R. admitted into hospital (sick)	MF
			1. O.R. evacuated (sick)	
	24/5/17		Company Training	
			2/LIEUT. G. E. SHEDD. joined Company from base depot.	MF
			2 O.R. admitted into hospital (sick)	

2449 Wt. W14957/M90 750,000 1/16 J.B.C. & A. Forms/C.2118/12.

Instructions regarding War Diaries and Intelligence Summaries are contained in F. S. Regs., Part II. and the Staff Manual respectively. Title Pages will be prepared in manuscript.

WAR DIARY
or
~~INTELLIGENCE SUMMARY~~

No1 MACHINE GUN COMPANY *(Erase heading not required.)*

Army Form C. 2118.

Place	Date	Hour	Summary of Events and Information	Remarks and references to Appendices
In the field	25/5/17		Company Training	[illegible]
			1.O.R. evacuated (sick)	
"	26/5/17		Company entrained to move to new area.	[illegible]
			LIEUT. R.H. ROHDE admitted into hospital (sick) & evacuated to HEALLY C.C.S.	
"	27/5/17		Company detrained at GODEWAERSVELDE. marched to billets at Q.34.b.4.4 & Q.34.b.6.4. (Ref. MAP SHEET 27)	[illegible]
"	28/5/17		Company Training	[illegible]
"	29/5/17		Company Training	[illegible]
"	30/5/17		Company Training	[illegible]
			2/LIEUT. G.F. LOWDON joined Company from base depot.	
			1.O.R. evacuated (sick.)	
"	31/5/17		Company Training	[illegible]

[illegible]
Lieut + Adjt.

2449 Wt. W14957/M90 750,000 1/16 J.B.C. & A. Forms/C.2118/12.

WAR DIARY.

No.1. MACHINE GUN COMPANY.

1st. INFANTRY BRIGADE.

1st. DIVISION.

JUNE. 1917.

Instructions regarding War Diaries and Intelligence Summaries are contained in F. S. Regs., Part II. and the Staff Manual respectively. Title pages will be prepared in manuscript.

WAR DIARY

No1 MACHINE GUN COMPANY

~~INTELLIGENCE SUMMARY~~.

(Erase heading not required.)

Army Form C. 2118.

Vol 18

Place	Date	Hour	Summary of Events and Information	Remarks and references to Appendices
IN THE FIELD	1/6/17		Company Training	
"	2/6/17		Company Training	
"	3/6/17		Company Training	
"	4/6/17		Company Training	
"	5/6/17		Company Training	
"	6/6/17		Company Training	
"	7/6/17		Company Training	
"	8/6/17		Company Training	
"	9/6/17		Company Training	
"	10/6/17		Church Parade	
"	11/6/17		Company moved via CAESTRE, STAPLE, & MAISON BLANCHE. to billets in farm at N.30 a 7.4. (REF MAP BELGIUM & FRANCE SHEET 27)	
"	12/6/17		Company Training	
"	13/6/17		Company Training	
"	14/6/17		Company Training	
"	15/6/17		Company moved via ZUYTPEEN, ANGE. TO WORMHOUDT. Company billeted in houses in WORMHOUDT on BERGUE RD.	
"	16/6/17		Company moved via BERGUE. - TETEGHEM. TO ST MALO LE BAINS Company billeted on Sea Front Attached to 96TH BRIGADE.	

Army Form C. 2118.

WAR DIARY

No1 MACHINE ~~or~~ GUN COMPANY

~~INTELLIGENCE SUMMARY.~~

(Erase heading not required.)

Instructions regarding War Diaries and Intelligence Summaries are contained in F. S. Regs., Part II. and the Staff Manual respectively. Title pages will be prepared in manuscript.

Place	Date	Hour	Summary of Events and Information	Remarks and references to Appendices
IN THE FIELD	17/6/17		Company moved VIA ADINKERKE & LAPANNE to billets in DE ZEEPANNE.	WT
"	18/6/17		Company relieved 165th FRENCH REGT in the line, proceeding VIA COXYDE - OUST DUNKERQUE BAINS AND NIEUPORT BAINS. No1, 2 & 3 SECTIONS in second & third lines and No4 SECTION in coast line.	
			No1 SECTION under Lieut. G. M. W. Atkinson with 2/Lieut Lowdon on Right.	
			No2 " under Lieut. R. H. Rohde with 2/Lieut Shead in Centre	
			No3 " under Lieut. F. W. Mackenzie on Left.	
			No4 " under 2/Lieut Taylor for Coast Line.	
			GUN POSITIONS.	
			RIGHT SECTION: 2 in DUNE.1. 2 " " 2. — CENTRE SECTION: 2 IN PETIT POUSSET. 2 IN L'ORGE — LEFT SECTION: 2 IN EXTRÊME GAUCHE 2 IN MOULIN GALETTE.	
			COAST LINE SECTION: 2 IN MASQUE 2 IN CUISINE	
			HEADQUARTERS: COMPANY BOYAU. MICHEL; RIGHT SECTION DUNE.1.; CENTRE " PETIT POUSSET; LEFT " EXTRÊME GAUCHE; COAST " MASQUE	WT
			Relief completed by 3.AM. 19th JUNE 1917.	

A7092. Wt. W123 9/M1293. 750,000. 1/17. D. D & L. Ltd. Forms/C2118/14.

Instructions regarding War Diaries and Intelligence Summaries are contained in F. S. Regs., Part II. and the Staff Manual respectively. Title pages will be prepared in manuscript.

WAR DIARY

No1. MACHINE GUN COMPANY.

~~INTELLIGENCE SUMMARY~~.

(Erase heading not required.)

Army Form C. 2118.

Place	Date	Hour	Summary of Events and Information	Remarks and references to Appendices
IN THE FIELD	19/6/17		Trenches reconnoitred, positions checked, Stores completed &c.	
			HEADQUARTERS	
			COMPANY HEADQUARTERS now established in BOYAU L'ECLUSETTE	
			RIGHT SECTION " " " BOYAU MICHEL	
			LEFT " " " " BOYAU MICHEL	
			Situation:- Quiet generally - Shelling of NIEUPORT LES BAINS.	
"	20/6/17		Transport moved to COXYDE BAINS	
			Indirect fire on LOMBARTZYDE - BAINS, WESTENDE, PLAGE BAINS RD. and on GARE JUNCTION of light railway lines north of this road.	
			Situation Quiet	
"	21/6/17		Transport moved to CAMP LEFEVRE.	
			Indirect fire as yesterday	
			Heavy enemy bombardment of left sector, with artillery, minenwerfer and aerial torpedoes from 1 AM. to 1-45 AM. Three casualties near one of our extreme gauche positions.	
			Lieut Atkinson handed over to Lieut. Cowdon.	
			Lieut Mackenzie " " " 2/Lieut Shead	
			Lieut Atkinson and Mackenzie proceeded to 1st line.	
"	22/6/17		Making up trench Stores	
			Positions improved	
			Situation normal.	
			500 rounds fired at hostile aeroplane about midday	
			Trench Mortar bombardment during afternoon.	

A7092 Wt. W128 9/M1293 750,000. 1/17. D. D & I. Ltd. Forms/C2118/14.

Army Form C. 2118.

Instructions regarding War Diaries and Intelligence Summaries are contained in F. S. Regs., Part II. and the Staff Manual respectively. Title pages will be prepared in manuscript.

WAR DIARY

No1 MACHINE GUN COMPANY

~~INTELLIGENCE SUMMARY.~~

(*Erase heading not required.*)

Place	Date	Hour	Summary of Events and Information	Remarks and references to Appendices
IN THE FIELD	23/6/17		Transport moved to RINCK CAMP Large fire observed in WESTENDE during the morning ~~During the morning~~ "GAS ALARM" heard on right about 1-30 A.M. but no gas was observed.	[initials]
"	24/6/17		Relief No1 & 2 SECTIONS took over 8 POSITIONS on the right from No2 M.G.Coy No3 & 4 " divided left sector between them. GUN POSITIONS are now as follows. REF MAP SECRET EDITION 2 1/1000 No1 SECTION under 2/Lieut Lowdon No1. POSITION M. 16. c 2.5. 2 " M. 15. d 7.7. 5 " M. 22 a 1.6. 6 " M. 15. d. 8.2. SECTION. H.Q. M. 16. c 2.5. No2 SECTION under Lieut Mackenzie No3 POSITION M. 15. b 6.1. " 4 " M. 15. b 2.1. " 7 " M. 15. d 3.5. " 8 " M. 15. d 2.7. SECTION. H.Q. M. 15. d 2.7. No4 SECTION under 2/Lieut Taylor No9 POSITION M. 15. a. 6.2. (DUNE 1.) 10 " M. 15. a 4.4. 11 " M. 15 a. 3.8. (MOULIN GALETTE) 12 " M. 9. c. 2.1. (EXTREME GAUCHE) SECTION H.Q. M. 14. b 7.6.	[initials]

A7092 Wt. W125 9/M1293 750,000. 1/17. D. D & L. Ltd. Forms/C2118/14.

Instructions regarding War Diaries and Intelligence Summaries are contained in F. S. Regs., Part II. and the Staff Manual respectively. Title pages will be prepared in manuscript.

WAR DIARY
or
~~INTELLIGENCE SUMMARY.~~
(Erase heading not required.)

No 1 M.G. Coy

Army Form C. 2118.

Place	Date	Hour	Summary of Events and Information	Remarks and references to Appendices
IN THE FIELD	24/6/17		No3 SECTION under 2/Lieut Taylor No 13 POSITION M. 14 b. 7.8. (forward CUISINE) " 14 " M. 14. b. 0.5. (MASQUE) " 15 } " 16 } " M. 14. b. 7.6. SECTION H.Q. M. 14. b. 7.6. Lieut Rohde & 2/Lieut Shead proceeded to 1ST LINE Situation Normal 1ST BRIGADE now in Command of Line. Relief complete 7-0 P.M.	[illegible]
"	25/6/17		Company H.Q. now situated at R. 24. a. 2. 3. Lieut Rohde took over command of No2 SECTION from Lieut Mackenzie Lieut Mackenzie took over command of No3 SECTION from 2/Lieut Taylor. 2/Lieut Taylor remained in command of No4 SECTION. Situation Heavy shelling of NIEUPORT BAINS during morning otherwise situation normal.	[illegible]
"	26/6/17		Ammunition carried to guns Positions improved Range Cards made Situation Normal.	[illegible]
"	27/6/17		Situation Heavy enemy shelling commenced at 4. A.M. an continued until 11-0 A.M. Remainder of day normal. One gun & team of No3 SECTION badly shaken. This team was relieved at 11 P.M. by a team from the 1st line Repairs to emplacements, dug outs & trenches damaged by shell fire carried out	[illegible]

A7092 Wt. W128 9/M1293 750,000. 1/17. D. D & I. Ltd. Forms/C2118/14.

Army Form C. 2118.

Instructions regarding War Diaries and Intelligence Summaries are contained in F. S. Regs., Part II. and the Staff Manual respectively. Title pages will be prepared in manuscript.

WAR DIARY

No1 MACHINE GUN COMPANY

~~INTELLIGENCE SUMMARY.~~

(Erase heading not required.)

Place	Date	Hour	Summary of Events and Information	Remarks and references to Appendices
IN THE FIELD	28/6/17		Lieut Lister relieved by Lieut Taylor	
			2/Lieut Shead relieved by Lieut Gowdon.	
			All guns except one of No3 SECTION were relieved by teams from 1st Line.	[initials]
			Relief reported complete at 2-30 A.M. on 29/6/17	
			Situation Normal	
"	29/6/17		Situation Normal	
			Work continued on all emplacements etc. damaged by shell fire	[initials]
"	30/6/17		Situation Normal	
			Work continued on all emplacements	[initials]
			40,000 ROUNDS S.A.A. Carried up.	

[signature]

LIEUT. & ADJT.

No1 MACHINE GUN COMPANY

A7092 Wt. W123.9/M1293 750,000. 1/17. D. D & L. Ltd. Forms/C2118/14.

W A R   D I A R Y.

No.1.MACHINE GUN COMPANY.

1st. INFANTRY BRIGADE.

1st.DIVISION.

JULY.1917.

No 1 MACHINE GUN COMPANY.

WAR DIARY

~~INTELLIGENCE SUMMARY.~~

(Erase heading not required.)

Army Form C. 2118.

Vol 19

Instructions regarding War Diaries and Intelligence Summaries are contained in F. S. Regs., Part II. and the Staff Manual respectively. Title pages will be prepared in manuscript.

Place	Date	Hour	Summary of Events and Information	Remarks and references to Appendices
IN THE FIELD	1/7/17	JH	2/LIEUT. Shead relieved LT. Mohde. 2/LIEUT. Melville relieved 2/LIEUT. Shead. Half teams from 1st line relieved the guns. Relief complete 1-30AM. 2nd Heavy enemy shelling from 9-15AM to 3-30PM. Bakke & blinded emplacements for No 7 gun destroyed Concrete emplacement at No 14 badly damaged, and gun damaged, later replaced by a reserve gun No 15 & 16. Section H.Q. at M.14.b.7.6. damaged beyond repair H.Q. for this section now established at M.14.b.a.5.	
"	2/7/17	JH	Lively shelling throughout the day. Hostile aircraft over our lines about 5-30P.M. 1 O.R. wounded	
"	3/7/17	JH	No 11 & 12 GUNS in action during the raid made by 1st BLACK WATCH on the extreme right of enemy lines. Our guns fired from 1-29A.M. to 1-50A.M. on enemy line TRANCHEE' 3rd COLT. Lieut. Fisher was in charge of these guns. Very quiet except for light shelling during earlier part of raid. Gas alarm was sounded in our lines about 12-50A.M. but no gas was observed Company was relieved by 2nd MACHINE GUN COMPANY in the afternoon and evening. Relief complete 9-0P.M. Company returned to billets at Camp Lefevre. Transport moved to same Camp. 3 guns remained in line to take part in intended raid.	
"	4/7/17	JH	3 guns co-operated in raid by 8th ROYAL BERKS. REGT. at 1-30A.M. which did not succeed. These guns rejoined the Company during the morning. Company cleaned guns & camp.	
"	5/7/17	JH	Kit & spare parts inspection. No 2 & 3 SECTIONS placed at disposal of 3rd BRIGADE for purpose of coast defence.	

No1 MACHINE GUN COMPANY.

WAR DIARY
or
~~INTELLIGENCE SUMMARY~~.
(Erase heading not required.)

Army Form C. 2118.

Instructions regarding War Diaries and Intelligence Summaries are contained in F. S. Regs., Part II. and the Staff Manual respectively. Title pages will be prepared in manuscript.

Place	Date	Hour	Summary of Events and Information	Remarks and references to Appendices
IN THE FIELD	6/7/17	JH	Company Training. No2 SECTION under Lieut. Mohde moved to billets with No3 MACHINE GUN COMPANY at COXYDE BAINS.	
"	7/7/17	JH	Company Training.	
"	8/7/17	JH	Church Parades. No1 SECTION relieved No3 SECTION.	
"	9/7/17	JH	Company Training. Test alarm for sections on coast defence.	
"	10/7/17	JH	Company Training. Orders received about 10-0 P.M. from 3rd BRIGADE for Coast Defence Sections to stand by for orders, the enemy having attacked about 7-15 P.M. and driven our troops from the Eastern (bank) of the Canal. Orders received at the same time from the 1st BRIGADE to place 2 SECTIONS at the disposal accordingly. Lieut. G.H. Lister reported to Brigadier General Commanding 2nd BRIGADE & received orders for the 2 SECTIONS to be disposed in the Route ETIENNE i.e. road running N.W. through M.25.7 and to set up a barrage on the east side of the YSER CANAL from the coast to M.21.6.5.5 (REF. MAP NIEUPORT 12 S.W. 1. EDITION 1.A.) Lieut. G.H. Lister was in command of No4 SECTION with 2/LIEUT R.S. Melville & Lieut. F.W. Mackenzie was in command of No3 SECTION. The guns were in position at dawn on the 11th July. Communication was established with advance Brigade H.Q. NIEUPORT BAINS and the right & left Battalions. Orders were received from Brigade that guns were only to fire in case of S.O.S. Heavy Bombardment during the night, including gas shells. Box Respirators were worn.	

A7092 Wt. W1289/M1293 750,000. 1/17. D. D & L. Ltd. Forms/C2118/14.

No1 MACHINE GUN COMPANY.

WAR DIARY

or

~~INTELLIGENCE SUMMARY~~.

(*Erase heading not required.*)

Army Form C. 2118.

Instructions regarding War Diaries and Intelligence Summaries are contained in F. S. Regs., Part II. and the Staff Manual respectively. Title pages will be prepared in manuscript.

Place	Date	Hour	Summary of Events and Information	Remarks and references to Appendices
IN THE FIELD	11/7/17	JHS	Day normal, heavy bombardment at night.	
"	12/7/17	JHS	Heavy gas shell bombardment from 1-30AM. to 5-30AM. Box respirators were worn continuously.	
"	13/7/17	JHS	Day normal. About 10 p.m. S.O.S. flare sent up on left. Fire was opened by all the guns & kept up for about two hours. 16,000 rounds expended	
"	14/7/17	JHS	Inter-section relief. No1 SECTION under Lieut. R.W. Atkinson & Lieut. P. Ferrie, No2 SECTION under 2/Lieut. C. Shead, in the line. No3 & 4 SECTIONS in reserve for Coast Defence. The guns of No1 & 2 SECTIONS were taken forward during the evening to positions from which to co-operate in attack by 32nd DIVISION on our right. Positions of No1 SECTION guns M. 20 d. 14. No2 " " M. 20. d. 08	
"	15/7/17	JHS	At 1-15AM. 32nd DIVISION attacked enemy trench just south of CRIQUE DE LOMBARDZYDE in M. 22 a & b. Our guns gave harassing fire North & South of the Maison Pavé in M. 15. a. Fire was intense at first & then slackening, continued until dawn. The guns were then laid on the barrage line in the event of S.O.S. being sent up. Guns of No1 SECTION were laid on line from M. 15 d. 85. 85 to M16 a 1.1. Guns of No2 SECTION from this point to M. 16. a. 3½. 3½. At 10-0AM. these sections returned to positions near ROU LE EOLIENNE.	
"	16/7/17	JHS	No1 & 2 SECTIONS withdrawn from the line at 10. P.M. & rejoined the Company.	
"	17/7/17	JHS	Company moved via ADINKERKE and LA PANNE to BRAY DUNES (REF. MAP BELGIUM. 1/100000 DUNKERQUE)	
"	18/7/17	JHS	Company moved via DUNKIRK to LECLIPON CAMP. Transport ½ mile south of where DUNKERQUE main road leaves the map.	

A7092 Wt. W128 9/M1293 750,000. 1/17. D. D & L. Ltd. Forms/C2118/14.

No 1 MACHINE GUN COMPANY.

Army Form C. 2118.

WAR DIARY
or
~~INTELLIGENCE SUMMARY~~.
(Erase heading not required.)

Instructions regarding War Diaries and Intelligence Summaries are contained in F. S. Regs., Part II. and the Staff Manual respectively. Title pages will be prepared in manuscript.

Place	Date	Hour	Summary of Events and Information	Remarks and references to Appendices
IN THE FIELD	19/7/17	JS	No parades. Cleaning camp &c. 2 Guns posted for Coast Defence	
"	20/7/17	JS	Company Training	
"	21/7/17	JS	Company Training	
"	22/7/17	JS	Church Parades	
"	23/7/17	JS	Company Training	
"	24/7/17	JS	Company Training	
"	25/7/17	JS	Company Training	
"	26/7/17	JS	Company Training	
"	27/7/17	JS	Company Training	
"	28/7/17	JS	Company Training	
"	29/7/17	JS	Church Parades	
"	30/7/17	JS	Company Training	
"	31/7/17	JS	Company Training	

J. S. Snowball
Lieut & Adjt
No 1 Machine Gun Coy.

A7092 Wt. W128 9/M1293 750,000. 1/17. D. D & L. Ltd. Forms/C2118/14.

W A R   D I A R Y.

No.1.MACHINE GUN COMPANY.

1st.INFANTRY BRIGADE.

1st.DIVISION.

AUGUST.1917.

No 1 MACHINE GUN COMPANY

WAR DIARY

~~INTELLIGENCE SUMMARY~~

(Erase heading not required.)

Instructions regarding War Diaries and Intelligence Summaries are contained in F. S. Regs., Part II. and the Staff Manual respectively. Title pages will be prepared in manuscript.

Army Form C. 2118.

VR 20

Place	Date	Hour	Summary of Events and Information	Remarks and references to Appendices
IN THE FIELD	1/8/17		Holiday	
"	2/8/17		Company co-operated in Brigade scheme. LECLIPON CAMP closed.	
"	3/8/17		Company Training 2 O.R. admitted into Hospital	
"	4/8/17		Company Training	
"	5/8/17		Church Parades	
"	6/8/17		Company Training	
"	7/8/17		Company Training 1 O.R. admitted into Hospital	
"	8/8/17		Company Training	
"	9/8/17		Company Training	
"	10/8/17		Company Training 1. O.R. admitted into Hospital	
"	11/8/17		Company co-operated in Brigade scheme 1 O.R. admitted into hospital	
"	12/8/17		Church Parades	
"	13/8/17		Company Training 1. O.R. admitted into Hospital 2 O.R. rejoined from hospital	
"	14/8/17		Company Training and Brigade scheme 1 O.R. rejoined from hospital	
"	15/8/17		Company Training	

A7092 Wt. W128.9/M1293 750,000. 1/17. D. D & I. Ltd. Forms/C2118/14.

No 1. MACHINE GUN COMPANY

WAR DIARY
or
~~INTELLIGENCE SUMMARY~~.
(Erase heading not required.)

Army Form C. 2118.

Instructions regarding War Diaries and Intelligence Summaries are contained in F. S. Regs., Part II. and the Staff Manual respectively. Title pages will be prepared in manuscript.

Place	Date	Hour	Summary of Events and Information	Remarks and references to Appendices
IN THE FIELD	16/8/17		Company Training	[illegible]
"	17/8/17		Company Training	[illegible]
"	18/8/17		Company Training	[illegible]
"	19/8/17		Church Parades	[illegible]
"	20/8/17		Company Training	[illegible]
"	21/8/17		Company Training No 2 & 4 SECTIONS cooperated with 8TH ROYAL BERKS. and 1ST CAMERON HIGHLANDERS. respectively in tactical scheme.	[illegible]
			Company co-operated in Brigade night operations.	[illegible]
"	22/8/17		Company Training	[illegible]
"	23/8/17		Company Training. 1 O.R. rejoined from hospital.	[illegible]
"	24/8/17		Company Training.	[illegible]
"	25/8/17		1ST DIVISION inspected by General Sir H. Rawlinson. G.O.C. 4TH ARMY.	[illegible]
"	26/8/17		Church Parades 1. O.R. rejoined from hospital 1. O.R. admitted into hospital.	[illegible]
"	27/8/17		Company Training	[illegible]
"	28/8/17		Company Training	[illegible]
"	29/8/17		Company Training	[illegible]
"	30/8/17		Company Training	[illegible]
"	31/8/17		Company Training	[illegible]

[illegible signature]
Lieut & a/adjt
No 1 Machine Gun Company.

A7092 Wt. W128.9/M1293 750,000. 1/17. D. D & L. Ltd. Forms/C2118/14.

WAR DIARY.

No.1. MACHINE GUN COMPANY.

1st. INFANTRY BRIGADE.

1st. DIVISION.

SEPTEMBER. 1917.

No 1 MACHINE GUN COMPANY

Instructions regarding War Diaries and Intelligence Summaries are contained in F. S. Regs., Part II. and the Staff Manual respectively. Title pages will be prepared in manuscript.

WAR DIARY
or
~~INTELLIGENCE SUMMARY~~.

(*Erase heading not required.*)

Army Form C. 2118.

Vol 21

Place	Date	Hour	Summary of Events and Information	Remarks and references to Appendices
IN THE FIELD	1/9/17		Brigade Scheme	
"	2/9/17		Church Parades	
"	3/9/17		Company Training	
			1 O.R. rejoined from hospital	
"	4/9/17		Company Training	
"	5/9/17		Company Training	
"	6/9/17		Route March	
"	7/9/17		Company Training	
"	8/9/17		Brigade Scheme	
"	9/9/17		Church Parades	
"	10/9/17		Company Training	
"	11/9/17		Route March	
"	12/9/17		Company Training	
"	13/9/17		Company Training	
"	14/9/17		Company Training	
"	15/9/17		Company Training	

A7092 Wt. W125 9/M1293 750,000. 1/17. D. D & L. Ltd. Forms/C2118/14.

No 1 MACHINE GUN COMPANY

WAR DIARY

or

~~INTELLIGENCE SUMMARY~~.

(Erase heading not required.)

Army Form C. 2118.

Instructions regarding War Diaries and Intelligence Summaries are contained in F. S. Regs., Part II. and the Staff Manual respectively. Title pages will be prepared in manuscript.

Place	Date	Hour	Summary of Events and Information	Remarks and references to Appendices
IN THE FIELD	16/9/17		Church Parades	
	17/9/17		Company Training	
	18/9/17		Company Training	
	19/9/17		Brigade Scheme	
	20/9/17		Holiday	
	21/9/17		Route March	
	22/9/17		Brigade Scheme	
			Sports of Machine Gun Company, and attached Motor Machine Gun Batteries of 1st DIVISION.	
	23/9/17		Church Parades.	
	24/9/17		Company Training	
			1. O.R. admitted into hospital (sick)	
	25/9/17		Company Training	
			1. O.R. admitted into hospital (sick)	
	26/9/17		Brigade Scheme.	
	27/9/17		Holiday	
	28/9/17		Company Training	
	29/9/17		Company Training	
	30/9/17		Church Parades	

[illegible] Lieut + adjt
No 1 Machine Gun Company

WAR DIARY.

No.1. MACHINE GUN COMPANY.

1st. INFANTRY BRIGADE.

1st. DIVISION.

OCTOBER. 1917.

No. 1. MACHINE GUN COMPANY.

WAR DIARY
or
~~INTELLIGENCE SUMMARY.~~
(Erase heading not required.)

Army Form C. 2118.

Instructions regarding War Diaries and Intelligence Summaries are contained in F. S. Regs., Part II. and the Staff Manual respectively. Title pages will be prepared in manuscript.

Vol 22

Place	Date	Hour	Summary of Events and Information	Remarks and references to Appendices
IN THE FIELD	1/10/17		Company Training.	
	2/10/17		Company Training	
	3/10/17		Company Training	
	4/10/17		Company Training.	
	5/10/17		Company Training.	
	6/10/17		Company Training. Inspection by Brigadier General A. J. Reddie D.S.O. Commanding 1st Infantry Brigade	
	7/10/17		Church Parades.	
	8/10/17		Company Training	
	9/10/17		Company Training	
	10/10/17		Company Training	
	11/10/17		Company Training	
	12/10/17		Company Training.	
	13/10/17		Company Training.	
	14/10/17		Church Parades	
	15/10/17		Company Training. 1 O.R. admitted into hospital (sick)	
	16/10/17		Company Training.	

A7092 Wt. W1238/9/M1293 750,000. 1/17. D. D & L. Ltd. Forms/C2118/14.

No 1 MACHINE GUN COMPANY

Instructions regarding War Diaries and Intelligence Summaries are contained in F. S. Regs., Part II. and the Staff Manual respectively. Title pages will be prepared in manuscript.

WAR DIARY

or

~~INTELLIGENCE SUMMARY~~.

(Erase heading not required.)

Army Form C. 2118.

Place	Date	Hour	Summary of Events and Information	Remarks and references to Appendices
IN THE FIELD	17/10/17		Company Training	
			1 O.R. admitted into hospital (sick)	
			1 O.R. rejoined from hospital	
	18/10/17		Company Training	
			3 O.R. evacuated to C.C.S. (sick)	
	19/10/17		Company Training	
	20/10/17		Company Training	
	21/10/17		Company moved via MARDICK – MOULIN SPICKER – GD MILLE-BRUGGHE – TO BILLETS at T 23 c 3 6. REF. MAP SHEET 19	
			Company inspected on march by Major General C. P. Strickland C.B. C.M.G. D.S.O.	
	22/10/17		Company moved via LE CLOCHE / LEDRINGHEM to billets at C.27.b.7.3. REF. MAP SHEET 27	
	23/10/17		Cleaning Camp & billets	
			Company Training	
	24/10/17		Company Training	
	25/10/17		Company Training	
			1 O.R. admitted into hospital (sick)	
			1 O.R. evacuated (sick) to C.C.S.	
	26/10/17		Company moved via WORMHOUDT – HERZEELE to billets at 7.29.d.7.2. REF. MAP SHEET 27	
	27/10/17		Cleaning Camp and Billets –	
			Company Training	
			1 O.R. admitted into hospital (sick)	
	28/10/17		Church Parades	
			1 O.R. admitted into hospital (sick)	

A7092. Wt. W128 9/M1293 750,000. 1/17. D. D & I. Ltd. Forms/C2118/14.

101 MACHINE GUN COMPANY

Army Form C. 2118.

WAR DIARY
or
~~INTELLIGENCE SUMMARY.~~

(Erase heading not required.)

Instructions regarding War Diaries and Intelligence Summaries are contained in F. S. Regs., Part II. and the Staff Manual respectively. Title pages will be prepared in manuscript.

Place	Date	Hour	Summary of Events and Information	Remarks and references to Appendices
IN THE FIELD	29/10/17		Company Training	
	30/10/17		Company Training	
			1 O.R. admitted to hospital (sick)	
	31/10/17		Company Training	

[illegible]
Lieut & adjt
101 Machine Gun Company.

A7092 Wt. W125 9/M1293 750,000. 1/17. D. D. & L. Ltd. Forms/C2118/14.

WAR DIARY.

No.1.MACHINE GUN COMPANY.

1st.INFANTRY BRIGADE.

1st.DIVISION.

NOVEMBER 1917.

No 1 MACHINE GUN COMPANY

1 MG Coy

Vol 23

Army Form C. 2118.

WAR DIARY
or
~~INTELLIGENCE SUMMARY.~~
(Erase heading not required.)

Instructions regarding War Diaries and Intelligence Summaries are contained in F. S. Regs., Part II. and the Staff Manual respectively. Title pages will be prepared in manuscript.

Place	Date	Hour	Summary of Events and Information	Remarks and references to Appendices
IN THE FIELD	1/11/17		Company Training	J. S. T.
"	2/11/17		Company Training	J. S. T.
"	3/11/17		Company Training	J. S. T.
			2/Lieut. Burn & 36 O.R. proceeded to IRISH FARM to act as carrying party	
"	4/11/17		Church Parades	J. S. T.
"	5/11/17		Company Training	J. S. T.
"	6/11/17		Company moved via HOUTKERQUE – WATOU – ST JAN TER BIEZEN to billets in School Camp at L.3.c.&d. (REF MAP SHEET 27)	J. S. T.
"	7/11/17		Cleaning Camp & Billets	J. S. T.
"	8/11/17		Company (less Transport) moved via Road Junction L.4.b. – SWITCH ROAD (REF MAP SHEET 27) entraining at RAILHOEK and detraining BRIELEN thence by road to JAMARE CAMP at B.27.c.&d. (SHEET 28) Transport moved via L.4.b. (REF MAP SHEET 27) SWITCH ROAD – BRANDHOEK – VLAMERTINGHE to lines at B.28.c.&d. (SHEET 28)	J. S. T.
"	9/11/17		Cleaning Camp & billets	J. S. T.
"	10/11/17		Cleaning guns, kit, &c. Fatigues at Transport lines.	J. S. T.
"	11/11/17		Belt filling, Cleaning gun kit.	J. S. T.
"	12/11/17		Belt filling	J. S. T.
"	13/11/17		Short Route March by sections.	J. S. T.

A7092' Wt. W128 9/M1293 750,000. 1/17. D. D & L. Ltd. Forms/C2118/14.

No 1 MACHINE GUN COMPANY.

WAR DIARY
or
~~INTELLIGENCE SUMMARY~~.

(Erase heading not required.)

Army Form C. 2118.

Instructions regarding War Diaries and Intelligence Summaries are contained in F. S. Regs., Part II. and the Staff Manual respectively. Title pages will be prepared in manuscript.

Place	Date	Hour	Summary of Events and Information	Remarks and references to Appendices
IN THE FIELD	14/11/17		Two Gun Teams from No 1 SECTION under 2/LIEUT. LOWDON relieved two teams of No 216. M.G. COY. in the line at YETTA HOUSES H.Q. Nos 3 & 4 SECTIONS moved to the Canal Bank via BRIELEN.	J. C. T.
	15/11/17		No 4 SECTION proceeded into the line under 2/LIEUT. MELVILLE at 6. A.M. & relieved a section of No 2 M.G. COY. at MEETCHEELE No 3 SECTION under 2/LIEUT. SHEAD with 2/LIEUT. BENSON relieved one section of No 2. M.G. COY. Two guns under 2/LT. BENSON at INCH HOUSES & two guns under Sgt Culley at BANFF HOUSE. 2/LIEUT LOWDON came out of the line to CANAL BANK after handing over his two teams to LT. STROYER of No 216. M.G. COY.	J. C. T.
	16/11/17		Nos 1 & 2 SECTIONS moved up to CANAL BANK. On the night of the 16/17th the 1st BRIGADE carried out two minor operations by surprise & captured VOCATION FARM some PILL BOXES, STRONG POINTS & 27 PRISONERS. All objectives were captured, except VIRILE FARM which was found to be very strongly held. One M.G. was also captured in VOCATION FARM. An attempt to regain the latter FARM two hours later was repulsed. M.G.s during these operations supplemented the Artillery S.O.S. barrage by firing bursts 500 yards beyond the objectives. The rate of fire was 200 rounds per minute, for the first two minutes, & then gradually brought down to 50 rounds per minute The four guns at MEETCHEELE fired 4000 rounds between them when the S.O.S. went up. & the two guns at BANFF HOUSE fired 3000 rounds between them on the SUNKEN ROAD. at V.23. b 45. 35. REF. MAP SPRIET. 1/10000. 2nd EDITION.	J. C. T.

A7092 Wt. W128 9/M1293 750,000. 1/17. D. D & I. Ltd. Forms/C2118/14.

No 1 MACHINE GUN COMPANY

Army Form C. 2118.

WAR DIARY
or
~~INTELLIGENCE SUMMARY.~~
(Erase heading not required.)

Instructions regarding War Diaries and Intelligence Summaries are contained in F. S. Regs., Part II. and the Staff Manual respectively. Title pages will be prepared in manuscript.

Place	Date	Hour	Summary of Events and Information	Remarks and references to Appendices
IN THE FIELD	16/11/17		During the whole tour of 48 hours these gun teams were heavily shelled by H.E. SHRAPNEL & GAS SHELLS.	J.S.T.
	17/11/17		Two gun teams from No 1 SECTION went up to YETTA HOUSES & were under the charge of LT. CARLISLE of No 216 M.G. COY. Two guns under Sgt Tindal at Thiel Battery were relieved the same day by two teams under Sgt. Grant.	J.S.T.
	18/11/17		No 2 SECTION under LT ROHDE relieved No 4 SECTION under LT MELVILLE at MEETCHEELE. 2/LT LOWDON relieved 2/LIEUTS. SHEAD & BENSON & took command of all four guns at BANFF HOUSE AND INCH HOUSES. On the night of the 18/19th the 1st BRIGADE carried out another operation & further advanced their line, capturing VIRILE FARM & several strong points. All objectives captured except VOX FARM. The M.G's carried out the same programme as in the operations on the night of the 16/17th.	J.S.T.
	19/11/17		No 3 & 4 SECTIONS moved back to DAMBRE CAMP from CANAL BANK. 2/LIEUTS. MELVILLE SHEAD & BENSON went back with them. The two guns at BANFF HOUSE were to be relieved today by the 35th DIVISION, but they did not manage to relieve till two days later owing to guides losing their way.	J.S.T.
	20/11/17		The Company was relieved by No 2. M.G. COY. in the line but H.Q & Nos 1 & 2 SECTIONS remained at CANAL BANK.	J.S.T.
	21/11/17		The Company moved to DAMBRE CAMP leaving the CANAL at 9 A.M.	J.S.T.
	22/11/17		The Company moved to the NEW AREA. Billeted at ST JANS TER BIEZEN moved at 12-30 P.M. in F.S.M.O. VIA SWITCH RD. road POPERINGHE through ST JANS. TER. BIEZEN to ROAD CAMP	J.S.T.

A7092 Wt. W128 9/M1293 750,000. 1/17. D. D & L. Ltd. Forms/C2118/14.

No 1 MACHINE GUN COMPANY

Instructions regarding War Diaries and Intelligence Summaries are contained in F. S. Regs., Part II. and the Staff Manual respectively. Title pages will be prepared in manuscript.

WAR DIARY

or

~~INTELLIGENCE SUMMARY~~.

(Erase heading not required.)

Army Form C. 2118.

Place	Date	Hour	Summary of Events and Information	Remarks and references to Appendices
IN THE FIELD	23/11/17		Company paraded by Sections to clean guns billets & limbers	J. C. T.
	24/11/17		Inspection of Guns & personnel kit.	J. C. T.
	25/11/17		Church Parades.	J. C. T.
			Bathing parade in the afternoon.	
	26/11/17		C. O's inspection in Fighting Order.	J. C. T.
			Inspection of Gas Helmets	
			Company Training	
	27/11/17		Company moved to NEW AREA near PROVEN. via the POPERINGHE – PROVEN Rd.	J. C. T.
			Moved at 1-15 P.M. in F.S.M.O. Billets in PLAISTOW FARM.	
	28/11/17		Cleaning billets	J. C. T.
	29/11/17		Cleaning Guns & billets	J. C. T.
	30/11/17		Company Training	J. C. T.

J. C. Taylor Capt
2nd Lt & Adjt.
No 1 M G Coy

A7092 Wt. W128 9/M1293 750,000. 1/17. D. D & L. Ltd. Forms/C2118/14.

W A R   D I A R Y.

No.1. MACHINE GUN COMPANY.

1st. INFANTRY BRIGADE.

1st. DIVISION.

DECEMBER. 1917.

No1 MACHINE GUN COMPANY

Army Form C. 2118.

Instructions regarding War Diaries and Intelligence Summaries are contained in F. S. Regs., Part II. and the Staff Manual respectively. Title pages will be prepared in manuscript.

WAR DIARY

or

~~INTELLIGENCE SUMMARY.~~

(Erase heading not required.)

Vol 24

Place	Date	Hour	Summary of Events and Information	Remarks and references to Appendices
IN THE FIELD	1/12/17		Company Training	P.S.T.
	2/12/17		Church Parades	P.S.T.
	3/12/17		Move to New Area. The Company marched to Proven Stn & proceeded by rail to BOESINGHE where it detrained & marched to billets (mostly dugouts) via YLAMERTINGHE. Billets at MARIE FARM	
			Nos 1 & 2 SECTIONS proceeded up the line at 3-0AM and relieved the French.	
			No1 SECTION. took over the right sector. Three positions two guns at each position Lieut Canning in charge.	
			No2 SECTION. took over the left sector. Three positions two guns at each position Lieut Rohde in charge.	P.S.T.
			Capt. Wemor took up his H.Q at ERISSEN HOUSE & took charge of eight guns from the 216 M.G COY.	

POSITIONS REF. SHEET BIXSCHOOTE.

RIGHT. LIEUT CANNING.			LEFT. LIEUT. ROHDE		
CÔTE VINGT.	U.11.a 1.3, 5.9.	2 GUNS.	CATINAT.	U.9.a. 15.55.	2 GUNS
CLOTHILDE	U.10.b. 15, 10.	2 GUNS.	ISLAND	U.8.b. 20.80.	2 GUNS
MANGELAERE.	U.10.a 45, 85.	2 GUNS.	PAPEGOED.	U.3.c. 20.55.	2 GUNS
SECTION. H.Q. MORTIER.	U.9.b. 25.35.		SECTION. H.Q. CATINAT.		

RESERVE No216. M.G COY.

LIEUT. CARR.	CEMETERY.	U.15.a. 80.32.	2 GUNS
	CHAMPAUBERT.	U.14.b. 90.45.	2 GUNS
LIEUT. CARLILE.	MONDOVI FARM	U.8.d. 20.10.	2 GUNS
	LES LILAS.	U.13.b. 75.90.	2 GUNS

A7092 Wt. W128:9/M1293 750,000. 1/17. D. D & L. Ltd. Forms/C2118/14.

No 1 MACHINE GUN COMPANY

Army Form C. 2118.

WAR DIARY

or

~~INTELLIGENCE SUMMARY.~~

(Erase heading not required.)

Instructions regarding War Diaries and Intelligence Summaries are contained in F. S. Regs., Part II. and the Staff Manual respectively. Title pages will be prepared in manuscript.

Place	Date	Hour	Summary of Events and Information	Remarks and references to Appendices
IN THE FIELD	4/12/17		Advanced Company H.Q. moved to MONDOVI [?] FARM.	P.S.T.
			Lieut. Snowbake [?] joined the C.O at H.Q.	
			Sections out of the line. Cleaning billets, guns, spare parts & filling belts.	
	5/12/17		REAR H.Q. moved to CANAL BANK just N.W. of J.1. BRIDGE.	
			Two days rations sent up to the sections in the line taken up by limber as far as LANCIER X RDS. The carrying party composed of men who would proceed up the line at first relief, made a second journey with S.A.A.	P.S.T.
			Lieuts Lowdon & Shead reconnoitred the line in the evening.	
	6/12/17		A composite team from No 3 & 4 SECTIONS under Cpl Kellow [?] with water took over a gun from the 54th Bde at FAIDHERBE X ROADS (BIXSCHOOTE U.5a.37.35)	
			Hot tea was carried to the sections in the line twice daily from this date. e.g. to be at LANCIER X ROADS at 3-30 AM & 4 PM.	P.S.T.
			Sections out of the line Cleaning guns & billets	
			Filling Belts	
			Improving duck board walks	
	7/12/17		Nos 3 & 4 SECTIONS under Lieuts Lowdon & Shead relieved Nos 1 & 2 SECTIONS in the line. They took two days rations with them & carried S.A.A. as well	P.S.T.
	8/12/17		Half Company out of the line at rest. Trench feet regulations	P.S.T.
	9/12/17		Half Company moved to CANAL HOUSE	P.S.T.
			Cpl Turve [?] & 4 men relieved Cpl Kellow [?] & his team at FAIDHERBE	
	10/12/17		Half Company on fatigue carrying rails for R.E.	P.S.T.
	11/12/17		The Company was relieved by No 3. M.G.Coy in the line & moved to billets at MARIE FARM.	P.S.T.

A7092 Wt. W123_9/M1293 750,000. 1/17. D. D & I. Ltd. Forms/C2118/14.

No 1 MACHINE GUN COMPANY

Army Form C. 2118.

WAR DIARY

or

~~INTELLIGENCE SUMMARY~~.

(Erase heading not required.)

Instructions regarding War Diaries and Intelligence Summaries are contained in F. S. Regs., Part II. and the Staff Manual respectively. Title pages will be prepared in manuscript.

Place	Date	Hour	Summary of Events and Information	Remarks and references to Appendices
IN THE FIELD	12/12/17		Company Cleaning Billets & equipment Inspection of Boots & Clothing.	J.S.T.
	13/12/17		Company moved to ZUIJHUIS CAMP VIA WOESTEN.	J.S.T.
	14/12/17		Company Training	J.S.T.
	15/12/17		Company Training	J.S.T.
	16/12/17		Company attended delousing Baths. No Church parades.	J.S.T.
	17/12/17		Company Training	J.S.T.
	18/12/17		Company Training C.O.s Inspection Ceremonial Parade	J.S.T.
	19/12/17		Ceremonial Parade for the Presentation of Medal Ribbons by G.O.C. 1st DIVISION. The C.O. LTS. CANNING AND MACKENZIE, C.S.M. Q.M.S. & 80 O.R. paraded Recipients of medals in this Company were:- No 20720 CPL TURVEY " 67720 PTE MAYALL " 57901 " TOTHILL } MILITARY MEDAL. The remainder of the Company on fatigue	J.S.T.
	20/12/17		Company Training.	J.S.T.

A7092 Wt. W128 9/M1293 750,000. 1/17. D. D & L. Ltd. Forms/C2118/14.

No1 MACHINE GUN COMPANY

Army Form C. 2118.

WAR DIARY
or
~~INTELLIGENCE SUMMARY~~.
(*Erase heading not required.*)

Instructions regarding War Diaries and Intelligence Summaries are contained in F. S. Regs., Part II. and the Staff Manual respectively. Title pages will be prepared in manuscript.

Place	Date	Hour	Summary of Events and Information	Remarks and references to Appendices
IN THE FIELD	21/12/17		Company moved to MARIE FARM via WOESTEN at 2-15 P.M. Cpl Waugh & two gun teams of 4 men each relieved two "A.A" guns of No2 M.G.COY at CANAL BANK between HETSAS and J.1. BRIDGE Transport lines N.W. of WOESTEN.	P.S.T.
	22/12/17		Company Training	P.S.T.
	23/12/17		Church Parades. Inspection of billets by C.O.	P.S.T.
	24/12/17		Company Training	P.S.T.
	25/12/17		Church Parades.	P.S.T.
	26/12/17		Company Training	P.S.T.
	27/12/17		The Company relieved No2 M.G.COY in the line No3 SECTION relieved the 7 right guns. Lieut Mackenzie in charge of MANGELAERE and LONELY MILL (4 guns) 2/Lieut Benton in charge of HILL 20. and FAIDHERBE (3 guns) No4 SECTION under Lieut Melville relieved the six left guns. The eight guns of No216 M.G.COY came under the Company's command Two "A.A" guns at CANAL BANK were relieved by No3 M.G.COY. Rear H.Q. at Canal Bank. Relief complete reported about 8-0 P.M. The line was very quiet.	P.S.T.
	28/12/17		Indirect fire from CATINAT, ISLAND and LONELY MILL Burst of 50 rounds at odd intervals Situation very quiet. Sections at CANAL HOUSE Cleaning guns & billets	P.S.T.

A7092 Wt. W128 9/M1293 750,000. 1/17. D. D & I. Ltd. Forms/C2118/14.

No1 MACHINE GUN COMPANY

Army Form C. 2118.

WAR DIARY

or

~~INTELLIGENCE SUMMARY~~.

(Erase heading not required.)

Instructions regarding War Diaries and Intelligence Summaries are contained in F. S. Regs., Part II. and the Staff Manual respectively. Title pages will be prepared in manuscript.

Place	Date	Hour	Summary of Events and Information	Remarks and references to Appendices
IN THE FIELD	29/12/17		Indirect fire from CATINAT AND LONELY MILL.	J. C. T.
			S.O.S. went up on the right Division Front.	
			All guns for Indirect fire were firing on S.O.S LINES in less than one minute.	
			About 5.000 rounds were fired.	
			Heavy bombardment on the right.	
	30/12/17		Indirect fire as usual.	J. C. T.
			Quiet on the line.	
			Every available man attended Pedicurium near CARPENTERS X ROADS CANAL HOUSE	
	31/12/17		Nos 3 & 4 SECTIONS relieved by No1 & 2 SECTIONS.	J. C. T.
			No1 SECTION on the right under Lieut Canning & Lieut Lowdon.	
			No2 SECTION on the left under 2/Lieut Melville, who was relieved 1/1/18 by 2/Lieut Bell.	

J. C. Taylor
2/LIEUT. & ADJT.
No1 MACHINE GUN COMPANY.

A7092 Wt. W128 9/M1293 750,000. 1/17. D. D & L. Ltd. Forms/C2118/14.

1ST DIVISION
1ST INFY BDE

NO. 1 MACHINE GUN COY.

JAN - FEB 1918

Instructions regarding War Diaries and Intelligence Summaries are contained in F. S. Regs., Part II. and the Staff Manual respectively. Title pages will be prepared in manuscript.

KOI Machine Gun Company

WAR DIARY

or

~~INTELLIGENCE SUMMARY.~~

(Erase heading not required.)

Army Form C. 2118.

Vol 25

Place	Date	Hour	Summary of Events and Information	Remarks and references to Appendices
In The Field	1.1.18		Indirect fire carried out during the night on tracks and bridges in rear of enemys lines. 2000 rounds fired. SOS was sent up at 5.20am by the Division on our left. Very heavy artillery fire from 5.20 - 6 am on the left. Slight shelling of PAPEGOED	J. C. J.
			REAR HQ. Attending Pediculium. Ration party at 3.15 pm	
"	2.1.18		Indirect fire from 5.30am to 6 am. 1000 rounds. HILL 20 and LONELY MILL shelled. Enemy M.G's during the night active on FAIDHERBE X ROADS.	J. C. J.
"	3.1.18		Harassing fire carried out on tracks in rear of enemy's line. Hostile artillery inactive. One EA flew over our lines and fired a few rounds into the front area.	J. C. J.
"	4.1.18		Company relieved by No 3 MG Coy and moved to TRENCH CAMP	J. C. J.
	5.1.18		Cleaning guns and billets	J. C. J.
	6.1.18		Company moved via WOESTEN to ZUIDHUIS "C" CAMP	J. C. J.
	7.1.18		Company Training. Lecture by Gas Officer (Bde). Two "AA" Guns mounted at Bde Hqrs.	J. C. J.
	8.1.18		Company Training	J. C. J.
	9.1.18		Route March via EYKHOEK & St SIXTHE	J. C. J.
	10.1.18		Company Training. FGCM. Sgt McKay D.	J. C. J.

A7092 Wt. W12839/M1293 750,000. 1/17. D. D. & L. Ltd. Forms/C2118/14.

No 1 Machine Gun Company

WAR DIARY

or

~~INTELLIGENCE SUMMARY.~~

(Erase heading not required.)

Army Form C. 2118.

Instructions regarding War Diaries and Intelligence Summaries are contained in F. S. Regs., Part II. and the Staff Manual respectively. Title pages will be prepared in manuscript.

Place	Date	Hour	Summary of Events and Information	Remarks and references to Appendices
In the Field	11.1.18		Company Training. Lt ROHDE and signallers on Pigeon Course at WOESTEN	J. S. T.
"	12.1.18		Company Training. Lecture by Brig General GRANT. DSO to all officers & sergts on company training.	J. S. T.
"	13.1.18		Church Parades. Company bathed at 10th GLOSTERS. No 4 Section took over two AA guns at CANAL BANK	J. S. T.
"	14.1.18		Company moved to TRENCH CAMP	J. S. T.
"	15.1.18		Company training. 2/Lt Lowdon and 20 OR on fatigue at CORMORAN DUMP.	J. S. T.
"	16.1.18		Company training. Draining camp after heavy rains. Lt Belra and 20 OR on fatigue at CORMORAN DUMP.	J. S. T.
"	17.1.18		Camp improvement and training	J. S. T.
"	18.1.18		Company moved to billets at CYAILLE VANDAMME FARM owing to old billets being flooded out.	J. S. T.
"	19.1.18		Camp improvements.	J. S. T.
"	20.1.18		The Company relieved No 2 M G Coy in the line with 14 Guns. The new gun position being at VICTORY POST No 1 Section relieved FAIDHERBE and HILL 20 } Right Sector No 3 Section relieved MANGELAERE and LONELY MILL } Right Sector No 2 Section relieved CATINAT and PAPEGOED } Left Sector No 4 Section relieved ISLAND & VICTORY } Left Sector No 1 Section under 2/Lt Benson, No 3 Section under Lt Mackenzie, Nos 2 & 4 Sections under 2/Lt Belra	J. S. T.

No 1 Machine Gun Company

WAR DIARY

or

~~INTELLIGENCE SUMMARY.~~

(Erase heading not required.)

Army Form C. 2118.

Instructions regarding War Diaries and Intelligence Summaries are contained in F. S. Regs., Part II. and the Staff Manual respectively. Title pages will be prepared in manuscript.

Place	Date	Hour	Summary of Events and Information	Remarks and references to Appendices
In the Field	20.1.18		The Company attended the Black Watch footwashing shed before going into the line.	J. S. Y.
"	21.1.18		The AA gun at LANNES COPSE (of the 216th M G Coy) fired 350 rounds at E A about 11.30am	
			Situation quiet except for some shelling of LONELY MILL with 5.9's	J. S. Y.
			REAR HQ. Cleaning and improving billets.	
"	22.1.18		No operations. Situation normal except slight enemy MG activity at PAPEGOED and VICTORY	
			Rear H Qrs. All men attended the Pediculium in the morning. Construction of new dug out. Carrying up rations in the evening. Fatigue party of 10 men from 1st SWB.	J. S. Y.
"	23.1.18		Operations Nil. Situation Normal.	
			Rear HQrs. Construction of new dug out with help of fatigue party of 10 men from No 3 M G Coy.	J. S. Y.
"	24.1.18		FAIDHERBE, LONELY MILL, PAPEGOED & VICTORY teams were completely relieved. Situation normal. Operations LONELY MILL guns fired 500 rds in retaliation on hostile MG's firing on FAIDHERBE X ROADS and HILL 20.	J. S. Y.
			Rear HQ. All men attended Pediculium. Construction of dug out.	
"	25.1.18		Operations. One gun at LONELY MILL fired 1500 rounds on enemy MG's.	J. S. Y.
			Situation normal.	
			Rear HQ. All men down from the line attended Pediculium.	

A7092 Wt. W128.9/M1293 750,000. 1/17. D. D & L. Ltd. Forms/C2118/14.

201 Machine Gun Company

WAR DIARY
or
~~INTELLIGENCE SUMMARY.~~
(Erase heading not required.)

Army Form C. 2118.

Instructions regarding War Diaries and Intelligence Summaries are contained in F. S. Regs., Part II. and the Staff Manual respectively. Title pages will be prepared in manuscript.

Place	Date	Hour	Summary of Events and Information	Remarks and references to Appendices
In the Field	26.1.18		Operations. One gun Lonely Mill fired 150 rounds on enemy MG's Rear H Q. Sandbagging new dug out	J. S. T.
"	27.1.18		Operations. One gun LONELY MILL fired 150 rounds on enemy MG's Rear H Q. Carrying sandbags to new dug out.	J. S. T.
"	28.1.18		Company relieved in the line by 94th M. G. Coy. and moved to billets at CYRILLE VANDAMME FARM	J. S. T.
"	29.1.18		Cleaning guns equipment billets etc. Inspection of iron rations, small kit, boots and clothing.	J. S. T. J. S. T.
"	30.1.18		Company moved to ZUIDHUIS FARM. 10.30am via WOESTEN.	J. S. T.
"	31.1.18		Checking and cleaning guns and gun kit.	

A7092 Wt. W128 9/M1293 750,000. 1/17. D. D & I. Ltd. Forms/C2118/14.

No 1 Machine Gun Company

Army Form C. 2118.

WAR DIARY
or
~~INTELLIGENCE~~ SUMMARY.
(*Erase heading not required.*)

Instructions regarding War Diaries and Intelligence Summaries are contained in F. S. Regs., Part II. and the Staff Manual respectively. Title pages will be prepared in manuscript.

Vol 26

Place	Date	Hour	Summary of Events and Information	Remarks and references to Appendices
In the Field	1/2/18		Company training. All officers attended lecture on work of RFC at Black Watch	[initials]
" " "	2/2/18		Church Parades. Hqrs. in afternoon (2 pm)	[initials]
" " "	3/2/18		Company training	[initials]
" " "	4/2/18		Company training	[initials]
" " "	5/2/18		Company training. Lecture to Officers and NCO's on AA work - Lieut Rolde	[initials]
" " "	6/2/18		Company training. Lecture to Officers and NCO's on "Points of the Horse" - Lieut Dukes	[initials]
" " "	7/2/18		Company training	[initials]
" " "	8/2/18		Company training	[initials]
" " "	9/2/18		Company moved into support in POELCAPELLE sector. Billets at CANAL BANK. Transport at SIEGE JUNCTION. No 3 Section relieved two AA guns at CANAL BANK, taking over from 35th Division. Lieut J S Snowball (2nd in Command) left to take command of No 2 M G Company	[initials]
" " "	10/2/18		Cleaning guns and limbers. Section parades	[initials]
" " "	11/2/18		Company training. Lieut A Dukes appointed 2nd in Command vice Lieut J S Snowball	[initials]
" " "	12/2/18		Fatigues and training	[initials]
" " "	13/2/18		Fatigues and training	[initials]
" " "	14/2/18		Fatigues and training	[initials]
" " "	15/2/18		Fatigues and training	[initials]
" " "	16/2/18		Fatigues and training. Baths in afternoon	[initials]
" " "	14/2/18		Church parades. Officers of Nos 1, 2 & 3 Sections reconnoitred line	[initials]

A7092 Wt. W125.9/M1293 750,000. 1/17. D. D & L. Ltd. Forms/C2118/14.

No1 Machine Gun Company

Instructions regarding War Diaries and Intelligence Summaries are contained in F. S. Regs., Part II. and the Staff Manual respectively. Title pages will be prepared in manuscript.

WAR DIARY

or

~~INTELLIGENCE SUMMARY.~~

(Erase heading not required.)

Army Form C. 2118.

Place	Date	Hour	Summary of Events and Information	Remarks and references to Appendices
In the Field	18.2.18		Fatigues	
"	19.2.18		Company training	[illegible]
"	20.2.18		Fatigues. Lecture to officers on German Gas at ELVERDINGHE. 3pm	[illegible]
"	21.2.18		Company relieved No2 M G Company in the line in POELCAPELLE sector. Transport at SIEGE JUNCTION. Coy HQ at CALIFORNIA dug outs. No1 Section (Lieut Canning) relieved BANFF (2 guns) and VACHER (4 guns) on right. No3 Section Lieut Mackenzie) relieved GLOSTER (2 guns) and DELTA (2 guns) HOUSES in the centre (Guns at DELTA relieved 2 guns of No216 M G Coy). No2 Section (Lieut Rohde) relieved BREWERY (1 gun) COURAGE (1 gun) and NORFOLK (4 guns) all in the vicinity of POELCAPELLE. 16 Guns in the line. Relief passed off quietly: no casualties. No4 Section (Lieut Shead) in reserve at Coy HQ	[illegible]
"	22.2.18		Situation normal. Operations nil. Work on new emplacements.	[illegible]
"	23.2.18		2 Guns at VACHER fired 500 rounds each on area V15a 45 10 in retaliation for enemy M G fire. Situation quiet. (Ref Sheet B1 Westroosebeke)	[illegible]
"	24.2.18		Normal. 2 guns DELTA fired 1500 rounds on HINTON V21 B.5.1. 4 Guns at NORFOLK fired 2800 rounds on SPIDER CROSS area.	[illegible]
"	25.2.18		2 Guns at VACHER fired 1000 rounds on V15.a 45 10 and neighbourhood. Enemy planes were fired on from COURAGE	[illegible]
"	26.2.18		2 Guns at VACHER fired 1000 rounds on region about V16.d 0.0. AA Gun at COURAGE fired 2450 rounds on enemy aeroplanes during the afternoon. AA guns at NORFOLK fired 1450 rounds at enemy planes. 4 guns at NORFOLK fired 1000 rounds on area V15 a 9.4	[illegible]

A7092 Wt. W128 9/M1293 750,000. 1/17. D. D & L. Ltd. Forms/C2118/14.

Instructions regarding War Diaries and Intelligence Summaries are contained in F. S. Regs., Part II. and the Staff Manual respectively. Title pages will be prepared in manuscript.

No 1 Machine Gun Company

WAR DIARY
or
~~INTELLIGENCE SUMMARY.~~
(Erase heading not required.)

Army Form C. 2118.

Place	Date	Hour	Summary of Events and Information	Remarks and references to Appendices
In the Field	24.2.18		Intersection relief :- Officers Lieuts Bebra, Saylor, Skead relieved Canning, Mackenzie, Rohde. No 4 Section (2 Lt Skead) relieved No 2 Section in left sector (POELCAPELLE). No 3 Section gun teams relieved each other in centre sector (GLOSTER & DELTA). Composite teams of remainder of company under 2/Lt Bebra relieved No 1 Section in right sector (BANFF HOUSES, VACHER FARM). Major Fitzwilliams, 2nd Welsh Guards & M G C was on this date attached to the company for instruction	JM.
"	28.2.18		2 Guns at NORFOLK fired on V14 b 95 80. 2 guns at NORFOLK fired on V15 a 8 0 3500 rounds were fired in all. 2 Guns at VACHER FARM fired 1000 rounds on area V22 a 55 05. Hostile artillery activity slightly above normal. This is probably accounted for by the raids carried out by friendly troops on our left. 250 rounds were fired by AA gun at NORFOLK on hostile aircraft. Lieut Dukes left the company for months leave to UK	JM.

[signature] Capt
Bde Major
1st Bde

A7092 Wt. W128 9/M1293 750,000. 1/17. D. D & L. Ltd. Forms/C2118/14.

www.ingramcontent.com/pod-product-compliance
Lightning Source LLC
Chambersburg PA
CBHW081409160426
43193CB00013B/2137

9781474502634